# PROPHETS, HEALERS, AND THE EMERGING CHURCH

# PROPHETS, HEALERS, AND THE EMERGING CHURCH

JOHN AND PAULA SANDFORD

**Destiny Image® Publishers, Inc.**
**P.O. Box 310**
**Shippensburg, PA 17257-0310**

"Speaking to the Purposes of God for This Generation
and for the Generations to Come"

ISBN 0-7684-2168-3

For Worldwide Distribution
Printed in the U.S.A.

This book and all other Destiny Image, Revival Press, MercyPlace,
Fresh Bread, Destiny Image Fiction, and Treasure House books
are available at Christian bookstores and distributors worldwide.

For a U.S. bookstore nearest you, call **1-800-722-6774**.
For more information on foreign distributors, call **717-532-3040**.
Or reach us on the Internet:

**www.destinyimage.com**

# ENDORSEMENT

May the Holy Spirit's fiery angels swirl around you as you read, and when you're into it, may you find it difficult to put the book down, as I did. In the end, I pray you may find yourself breathing fresh air, looking forward again with hope (rather than dread), anticipating life again—whether in the fires, on the shelf, or in the heights or spiritual warfare. Wherever He is, it's worth it; this is one of the grand themes of the book. God bless you as you read.

Donald L. Milam
Author, *Lost Passions*
and *The Ancient Language of Eden*

# CONTENTS

# About the Authors

John and Paula Sandford are co-founders of Elijah House, Inc., an international ministry established in 1974 in response to the Lord's calling in Malachi 4:5-6 and Matthew 17:11.

John and Paula have traveled extensively to conduct seminars on marriage and the family, inner healing and transformation, prayer, the gifts of the Holy Spirit, burden-bearing and intercession, small group ministry, leadership training, and other related subjects in gatherings sponsored by Protestant and Catholic groups and churches all over the world. They are also active in the renewal and reconciliation movements and have walked in the Holy Spirit since 1958. John and Paula have made numerous radio and television appearances in the United States, Canada and overseas. Several of their books are required reading in a number of colleges.

John graduated from theological seminary with an M.D. in Religion and Personality. For 21 years, he pastored churches in Illinois, Kansas, and Idaho, where Paula's leadership skills and involvement were focused on music and Christian education. For three years, she also taught English, Spanish and Idaho history in local Idaho high schools. From the time Elijah House was founded, Paula has teamed with her husband in ministry, and she was ordained in 1995.

John and Paula celebrated 50 years of marriage in 2001. They have six children, 20 grandchildren and 15 great-grandchildren.

Elijah House seeks to spread the word of restoration and reconciliation through prayer counseling, originating from its headquarters in Post Falls, Idaho, reaching out to the farthest regions of the world. They conduct teaching and healing seminars and offer training for effective prayer ministry to Christian lay leaders, pastors, and to professional counselors. Elijah House staff members are now accepting invitations to minister and teach in many nations. At this writing, Christian leaders from Austria, Canada, Finland, Australia and New Zealand have already established Elijah Houses in their own countries. Additional requests have come from several other nations.

Ministry materials are available through audio and video tapes and books (written primarily by the Sandford family), as well as additional resources by Elijah House prayer counselors and teachers.

# CHAPTER ONE

# JOHN'S EXCITING TIMES

Could there be a more exciting time in all of Christian history to be born anew and Spirit-filled than right now?!

When I was a boy, it seemed as if nobody knew anything about the Holy Spirit. Only a few "wild-eyed" emotional Pentecostals had any experience of the Holy Spirit—just enough to scare the rest of us "proper" Christians away from Him. The entire Church the world over had become the valley of scattered dry bones of Ezekiel 37. Almost every denomination was filled with hubris (spiritual pride). The Church was scattered. Each branch thought itself superior in revelation to every other. "Sorry, we've got the truth. You don't. We'll make it to Heaven; you won't." Semantically, *words* about God had become confused with God, and with reality itself. "Our grasp of truth is the only reality. Everybody else is in delusion and lost."

Yet, in my lifetime (I was born in 1929), we all have seen the Lord resurrect the dead and scattered bones of the Church!

## GATHERING THE SCATTERED BONES

*And I looked, and behold, **sinews were on them, and flesh grew, and skin covered them** (Ezekiel 37:8a, emphasis added).*

"Flesh grew" means that teachings have begun to flesh out the dry bare bones of the faith. In 1958 when I came into the Holy Spirit, there were very few books about the Holy Spirit or the gifts of the Holy Spirit among Protestant old-liners and none among the Catholic. It was a dry and arid desert. In the 44 years since that time, we have seen the Lord raise up hundreds of godly teachers, and thousands of books have flooded the barren market. The Lord is fleshing out His Body.

***"Sinews were on them."*** In the first 50 or more years of the twentieth century, the Church was weak and vacillating, struggling against the onslaughts of rationalism and scientific technology, trying merely to hang on to faith despite all that rationality said. But now the Church has arisen in power. Muscles have grown. Now the Church has raised up its own scientists who contend for the faith rather than against it, who employ scientific technology to support belief rather than dismantle it.

Nevertheless, the war is far from won. We are still the disrespected Cinderella among the sisters of science. Many scientists, especially evolutionists, continue to look down their noses and disregard whatever we say. But the Church is rising—like the fistfighter Rocky who, although battered and beaten up, comes on strong in the end and wins against all odds. Prophetically let me announce it: *In the end, science itself will prove the veracity of the Bible!* And philosophers will turn to defend the solid doctrines of faith.

> *No longer will the fool be called noble,*
> *Or the rogue be spoken of as generous.*
> *For a fool speaks nonsense,*
> *And his heart inclines toward wickedness,*
> *To practice ungodliness and to speak error against the Lord,*
> *To keep the hungry person unsatisfied*
> *And to withhold drink from the thirsty.*
> *As for a rogue, his weapons are evil;*
> *He devises wicked schemes*
> *To destroy the afflicted with slander,*
> *Even though the needy one speaks what is right.*
> *But the noble man devises noble plans;*
> *And by noble plans he stands.*
> Isaiah 32:5-8

Today the evolutionists, abortionists, homosexual activists, and modernistic liberals still hold center stage and claim the adherence of most of the populace. But I speak prophetically and triumphantly: That day will soon end! You and I are living in the day when the Lord is moving to reclaim His lost and prodigal world! Samsonite sinews are growing on the Body of Christ—and I am not referring to the popular luggage brand, but muscles of scholarship that won't be denied!

*"And skin covered them."* Christians who formerly could hardly wait to find loopholes in brothers' and sisters' thoughts and doctrines, in order to elevate themselves while putting others down, are turning around in repentance. God is teaching His people how to cover one another. The Body of Christ is growing its skin.

Thirty years ago the Catholic Bishop Topel of Spokane, Washington, permitted me as a Protestant pastor to be the spiritual director of nuns in his diocese! Previously unheard of, impossible only a few years earlier! We're covering one another. We are learning what Romans 12:16 means, that we should at all times, "Be of the same mind toward one another; do not be haughty in mind, but associate with the lowly. Do not be wise in your own estimation."

Paula and I have been in numerous meetings in which Roman Catholic and Protestant leaders have repented for opposing and disrespecting one another, while tears flowed and the glory of the Lord shone all around. What an exciting age! We're learning how to agree on the essentials and allow others to be different on the non-essentials.

Brother pastors and leaders across denominational lines are learning to submit to one another's scrutiny, learning how to cover one another in intercessory prayer and in forgiveness and reconciliation. I remember how, in the isolated and frozen small town of Haver, Montana, in weather sixty degrees below zero Fahrenheit, the pastors of that town met and confessed their need for each other. The Baptist pastor looked up with tears rolling down his face to say, "I'm all alone out here. My conference minister is too far away. I've got nobody to talk to." And then, pointing to the Catholic priest (who looked like Robin Williams and had his wonderful sense of humor), he said, "I'm gonna come to you. You're going to be my confessor and my priest!" There wasn't a dry eye in the place. The Church is growing skin! What an exciting time!

At the same time the Lord has been raising up the fivefold ministry of apostles, prophets, evangelists, pastors, and teachers. Wondrous as that is, we'll refrain from speaking about it here—we testify about that later throughout the book.

## DEMON CONCEPT VERSUS HUMAN LOGIC

Shortly after the Second World War, the Church succumbed to the siren song of pseudo-science, and bought into the idea that the bright light of human rationality would do away with the superstitious bugaboos of satan and demons. After all, these were "mere figments of imagination," only "psychological projections of evil." An example of this way of thinking is demonstrated by the popularity of Sir Arthur Conan Doyle's magnificent series of detective stories about Sherlock Holmes and his sidekick Watson, which were actually a trumpeting of the victory of cold, analytical, deductive reasoning over fear and superstition.

People had come to believe that the mind of mankind would become the new savior that would deliver us from the ragged world of fear and anxiety. Consequently, no Christian with any sense thought demons still had to be battled. We sent troubled people to psychiatrists and insane asylums. Almost no counseling could be found inside the Church. The Body of Christ had abdicated part of the ministry it should have done. (Because of this, Paula and I and scores of others pioneered inner healing and are restoring deep ministry to the Church, where it belongs, which we will discuss later in this book.)

In those days we used the word demons only figuratively, when we wanted to say for example that we were struggling with "the demons of our mind," unaware we were actually speaking factual truth. Nobody thought them real. However, in the last 40 years, the Lord has awakened the Church to reality. He has revealed that the actual myth was our own belief in the pseudo-science and consequent philosophy that there are no demons, and the reality is that we have been given power to exorcise them out of people's lives and dwelling places.

My son Mark and I wrote the book *A Comprehensive Guide to Deliverance and Inner Healing* to equip the Body with wisdom and power in the burgeoning ministries of deliverance and inner healing. Don Basham and Cindy Jacobs and others have written powerful books about deliverance. Today, most any charismatic Christian understands that demons are real and that we have the command and authority to displace them. Our prayer counselors at Elijah House, a ministry Paula and I co-founded in 1974, regularly cast demons out of those who come to be ministered to. What a vast transformation in a few short years!

## "HARMLESS" DABBLING IN THE OCCULT

Throughout the first half of the twentieth century the Church was almost totally naive and uninformed about occult practices and their dangers. Christians often read their horoscope in the morning paper, "just in case," and thought nothing of it, blithely unaware this was sin (see Is. 47:12-15). Christians went to "Aunt Fanny" to have their fortunes told or their palms read, and they enjoyed feeling goose bumps when the carnival's crystal-ball gazer happened to hit on something that sounded like it could apply. The Book of God's eternal Law had become lost from modern Christians' minds and hearts, akin to the Israelites in the day of good King Josiah. Ignorant of Deuteronomy 18:9-12, people plunged into the pitfalls of occult bondage and never knew those sins were a primary cause of their subsequent trials and troubles:

> *When you come into the land which the Lord your God is giving you, you shall not learn to follow the abominations of those nations. There shall not be found among you anyone who makes his son or his daughter pass through the fire, or anyone who practices witchcraft, or a soothsayer, or one who interprets omens, or a sorcerer, or one who conjures spells, or a medium, or a spiritist, or one who calls up the dead. For all who do these things are an abomination to the Lord, and because of these*

*abominations the Lord your God drives them out before you* (Deuteronomy 18:9-12 NKJV).

Many Christians went to seances to try to consult with departed family members, unaware this was deadly entrapping sin, utterly forbidden. Most often, if they contacted anything, it was a demonic familiar spirit who could perfectly mimic their loved ones' voices and tell secrets because the demon had watched over them during their lives!

However, in these last short 40 or 50 years, the Holy Spirit has revived the truths of God's Word in nearly every evangelical and charismatic Christian's mind and heart and reestablished the walls of conscience and protection. Today we are forearmed with the protection of God's Word (see Ps. 19:11).

Sometimes we take for granted or miss seeing stupendous miracles of transformation taking place before our eyes. However, I've lived long enough to know where we were during the first 60 years of the twentieth century, and I can attest to the tremendous redemption God has accomplished in such a few short years! What an exciting time!

## THE TRUTH ABOUT SECRET SOCIETIES

Until fairly recently, many Protestant and some Catholic Christians were members of the Masonic Order. In many mid-western towns, businessmen could hardly run their stores successfully if they were not Masons. Countless pastors joined, thinking this would be where they could meet and minister to their parishioners—and saw nothing wrong with it!

Now, the Lord, who has set about purifying His Church, as prophesied in Malachi 3, Isaiah 4, and hundreds of other places in the Scriptures, has revealed the satanic base of Masonry and its horrible descendancies of harm to the children and grandchildren of members (see Deut. 5:9). Any good Christian bookstore can find in its microfiche many enlightening and accurate books (too numerous to list here) about the defilements of the Masonic Order—and many other orders, such as the Elks Lodge. Evangelicals and charismatics are fleeing such snares of the devil, when only two decades or so ago they would have thought nothing of belonging to such clubs. How thankful we ought to be for the way God is maturing His Church and setting it progressively free from trap after trap!

## RESTORATION AND RENEWAL

We are now full into Isaiah 58:11-12 (NKJV):

*The Lord will guide you continually, and satisfy your soul in drought, and strengthen your bones; you shall be like a watered garden, and like a spring of water, whose waters do not fail. Those from among you shall build the old waste places; you shall raise up the foundations of many generations; and you shall be called the Repairer of the Breach, the Restorer of Streets to Dwell in.*

I believe, in all this restoration and renewal, perhaps the most important is the restoration of the fivefold offices—specifically, from my point of view, the apostolic and the prophetic. I discuss this throughout later chapters in this book. Suffice it to say here that the Church has been weak because its foundations have not been in place (see Eph. 2:19-22). One of the most exciting facts of life in Christ today is the resurrection of the offices of the prophet and the apostle in our time!

It has been Paula's and my calling to be forerunners in that glorious work. Our book, *The Elijah Task*, is now regarded by many as the basic classic in the prophetic field. We are not saying this to brag, unless it be upon our wonderful Lord, but to celebrate the glory of what God is doing in our time, and our own joy in being part of it.

The same is true about sanctification and transformation. When Paula and I began to resurrect the office of inner healing in the life of the Church, we found that not only had the office of healing been lost, so was any concept that inner troubles and evil practices could still remain in the hearts of born anew people—which need to be dealt with! The entire understanding of sanctification and transformation had devolved to trying harder to live like Jesus, despite great fractures and wounded places in the heart. No one knew the good news of change through the gospel of the inner man.

The Church was not being sanctified and transformed into the nature of Jesus, and tragically, the behavior of born anew Christians often shamed the name of the Lord and turned many away from Him. Striving by human strength and then inevitable guilt and failure had taken the place of restful ministry to the deep heart. Though these things are still too true today, now the gospel to the inner man is spreading joy and transformation across the land and into the Church at an ever-increasing rate.

It has been Paula's and my joy to be among the foremost forerunners in restoring both the office of the prophet and of sanctification and transformation in the life of the Church.

Many have asked us, "Where did you get all those insights that have become keys of knowledge to set so many free through inner healing?" Or, "How did you discover what it is to be a prophet when nobody knew anything about that in the modern day? Where did it all come from?"

The thing is: *We did not set out to find hidden truths; we set out to serve.* Along the way, whenever we came against a problem we couldn't solve, we said our usual fervent, righteous, and intellectual prayer, "Help!" And God answered. We simply listened to God. Our advice is: Don't try to find pearls of knowledge; try to find Him in service to Him. The Holy Spirit is the giver of truth. He gives it when we need it, while we're serving; seldom does He reveal it just because we want to know.

Ours is an incarnational faith. We hear through what we have experienced and what we have become. It is not as though we are pipes through which God might download truths untouched by what we are. Our hearing is colored by the many hues of our own personal nature. God has to use what is stored in our hearts and memory banks to talk *to* us or minister *through* us.

For example, when I was a boy there was no television. I whiled away many happy hours putting together jigsaw puzzles. Little did I know that in that simple play activity God was building into my mind the habit of looking for what did or didn't fit. Now that habit has become a daily practice of looking for the missing pieces in the puzzles of people's lives.

Hebrews 1:1-2 says, "God, after He spoke long ago to the fathers in the prophets in many portions and in many ways, in these last days has spoken to us in His Son, whom He appointed heir of all things, through whom also He made the world." Some have mistakenly proclaimed this Scripture to mean that since God now speaks through His Son, there is no longer any need for prophets. But our Lord also said that Scripture does not contradict itself, and throughout the New Testament the Lord continued to speak through His prophets and apostles. To me, this text means that since our Lord has come, there has consequently come a change in the way He speaks to and through us. In the Old, the Holy Spirit came upon men and women and they could speak for Him. But now the Holy Spirit resides within each believer. Now, God speaks in and through His Son resident within us.

In the Old it seemed as though the Lord simply popped a cassette into someone's mouth, pressed "play," and out came His message. Very little of the prophet's own nature was risked or involved in the process, compared to what happens in the New. The cross and the way of purification had not yet opened the way for deeply transformed character. Therefore, God would move mightily upon a prophet and overflow what he was, like a flood surging over a dam, until His word could come across as purely as possible. Prophets who erred were simply not enough under the power of God's Spirit.

But in the New a change has happened. God's Spirit now dwells within, and each prophet or prophetess speaks as a son or daughter, which means that God now risks to speak in and through His servants, in and through all they have become. The flood of His Spirit no longer has to overflow to find purity; it flows in and through each son and daughter, purified by the Lord.

So, if one asks, "How did Paula and you hear all that has become foundational for the office of the prophet and inner healing?" the answer is to be found in our histories, in our biographies, as the Lord built us into who and what we are. It is the same for every modern forerunner. Through all that John Wimber experienced, God built a man through whom He could pioneer the rediscovery of power evangelism, and the working of wonders. In Mike Bickle and Dutch Sheets' lives the Holy Spirit built two who could pioneer the rediscovery of prayers of intimacy and intercession. Through the struggles of his life, C. Peter Wagner was prepared by God to become an apostle among His prophets; Chuck Pierce and Cindy Jacobs were enabled to pioneer spiritual warfare. And so on for all His servants. *What we have lived through becomes the grist mill that refines and shapes our listening to God.* Perhaps it was somewhat so in the Old, but the difference in the New is the powerful effect of the cross, transforming all that we as Christians experience in depths and ways that were not available in the Old.

Incidentally, ours is the only religion rooted and told in actual down-to-earth history. Ours is the only faith in which God Himself has come to live among us on earth in history. The Bible is almost entirely history. The Bible is God's biography of His actions among us from Genesis to Revelation and is still relevant today because God doesn't change (see Heb. 13:8) and neither do people. Human beings are the same today as they were in the beginning. We simply have more complex veneers spread over the same base mix of Adamic sin and human goodness after God's image.

For these reasons, and more, when Destiny Image Publishers asked us to write a chronicle of the founding of inner healing and of the prophetic, we knew that we should write autobiographically because it is our personal history that shapes us and affects how we hear revelations from God. Goethe, the German poet, said of history, "Here at the roaring loom of time I ply, weaving for God the garment thou seest Him by." God shaped Paula and me at the loom of our personal histories to become the forerunners of the prophetic and of inner healing.

It is our hope as you read our frank confessions of our lives that you will see the hand of God in your own, that you will see His Master hand shaping you for whatever is His calling upon your own life. After all, that is the point of testimony, to spark in others revelations of themselves.

CHAPTER TWO

# JOHN'S LESSONS FROM EARLY CHILDHOOD

*Before I formed you in the womb I knew you, and before
you were born I consecrated you; I have appointed you a
prophet to the nations* (Jeremiah 1:5).

## MY MOTHER'S DREAM

In November 1928, my mother, Zelma Potter Sandford, had a
dream. In that dream, she drove to the old Potter family home-
stead at night. As the headlights swung across the garage, she saw a
great figure, sitting there, as though waiting for her. Frightened, she
ran for the back door. As she touched the screen, a great bolt of
power shot into her left shoulder and down through her body. She
said it felt like a thousand volts. A voice said, "Do not be afraid, for
I am God. You are to have a son, who will be My servant." The Lord
went on to tell her many things the son would do, so great they
frightened her terribly.

When she awoke from the dream she told my father about it.
He merely grunted sleepily. She found she could remember the
whole dream vividly, except for what her son was supposed to do.
The next day a visit to the doctor confirmed that she was indeed
pregnant. She had eight months to think about what she should do or
reveal about her dream. She decided it was best to tell no one except
my paternal grandmother. She especially thought it best not to tell
me; she only worked me harder as I grew older.

Having pioneered in the healing of prenatal experiences, I now
know that while I was growing in my mother's womb, I also heard
those commands, but both my mother and I were kept from remem-
bering. Seeds of recollection were planted that would guide me subliminally all my life, but the Lord in His wisdom knew it would be

best for neither of us to know concretely, lest that curtail the search I would need to undergo, and its consequent lessons of wisdom.

I enjoyed a normal, happy early childhood, though I would often draw apart and read the Bible, especially Books about the prophetic. I would hide in the attic, read, and think. Always in the back of my mind, I felt there was something impending on my life, and I had to find out what it was. That search eventually led me to the ministry God guided me into.

Looking back on that period of my life, I can see so many events and learning experiences that later affected and became an important part of my ministry. Sometimes God uses simple things, everyday experiences, to prepare us for His greater purposes to come.

## A LESSON THROUGH LINAMENT

Shortly after my birth in Joplin, Missouri, July 23, 1929, my parents took my older brother Hal and me with them to California. There my father studied a new form of therapy that combined chiro-practics, massage, and electro-neural patterning in the body. We were often his "patients" for practice. He had a piece of flat board about two feet square, on which white quarter-inch flat sticks had been imposed in the middle, across and down, which formed a cross. We would stand straddle of the cross, our insteps on the horizontal cross stick, with our feet on each side of the vertical stick about shoulder width. He had a plumb line, suspended from the ceiling be-hind us, along which he would sight the alignment of our backbone.

Using a soft wide pencil, he marked small X's at numerous places down our back. Then he would place us face down, one at a time, on a massage table that had a face hole, and lather us from head to toe with linament. It had a strong pleasant smell and stung a little but felt good. And then he would massage us, placing thumb pressure on the marked spots, until whatever soreness had accumu-lated was dissipated. Turning us over, he continued massaging until we had been rubbed down all over. It felt so good, and we loved to have him do it.

Years later I came to understand that God used those experiences to write into my heart many things: trust of the Father, expectancy that being examined would bring healing, willingness to try new things and expect good, ability to tolerate and enjoy being touched by others with "laying on of hands," etc. It's so interesting to discover how God uses such simple down-to-earth things in our earliest childhood to write onto our hearts things that will prepare us for His service in adulthood.

## ELEPHANTS AND EARTHQUAKES

We lived in southern California for the first four years of my life. And, of course, that area of the country is known for having earthquakes. Even though I was very young, I can still remember watching a huge hutch cupboard dance above me during an earthquake while my uncle Loren (from whom comes my middle name) rolled off the couch and under the piano!

I was four years old when the great earthquake of 1933 hit Los Angeles. My brother and I were playing in the yard, when suddenly, the quake slammed us to the ground. As we tried to get up, the yard waved like a wheat field in a mighty wind! Mother came outside to see if we were all right, and we immediately ran to her and hugged her. My brother cried out, "What was that?" She replied, "The elements were acting up." I thought she said the elephants were acting up! It was many years before I understood that elephants didn't cause earthquakes.

I can think of at least two events which taught spiritual lessons to my heart in those early years in California. On the day of the great earthquake, my father had an appointment to get a haircut, but he was detained and missed his scheduled time. Later he went to the shop and discovered that the roof had collapsed and filled the barber's chair with heavy bricks—exactly at the time he should have been sitting there. Even at four years of age, I knew God's providence had protected my father. Looking back I know that incident taught my young heart to trust God's power and protection.

Another event occurred at the beach. While my great-aunt Martha, my father's aunt, was visiting, we took her to see the ocean. She loved to stand and feel the tug of the sand and water as it came rushing past her, in and out. Perhaps barely four, I had no fear of the water and loved to stand beside her. But then, something special happened. While I was standing there, I felt the presence of the Lord come over me. The following second I was traveling west over the water at great speed. Most details of what happened next have been blanked from my memory; however, I did tell my parents I had been to China to talk with a lady there. They didn't scoff; they just chalked it up to the antics of their unusually imaginative child.

I came to understand the significance of that experience years later. For ten years, from 1958 to 1968, I worked with Agnes Sanford, from which liaison the forerunning task of inner healing began. (Notice, there's no middle "d" in her last name; we're not related.) Agnes grew up in China, the daughter of a Presbyterian missionary, and was still in China at the time. After I met her I remembered a few details of that childhood "visit" and knew I had checked in with her to say, "I'm here, let's do it." Agnes always felt that we had been predestined to meet and work together in inner healing.

(In the 1970s critics, who didn't know what they were talking about, labeled—actually libeled—Agnes Sanford with many false accusations, and she became the favorite whipping girl of the apologists of those days. Later on in this writing, I'll set the record straight. She was not at all what they thought she was!)

## A LESSON IN PERSONAL RESPONSIBILITY

Another incident wrote lessons on my heart. My brother Hal was in first grade at Easter time when someone had brought in hardboiled eggs for the children in his class to decorate and eat. Hal came home furious at Mom because she had never taught him how to break eggs against his forehead without getting egg yokes running down his face, as the other children could do!

I remember, vividly, thinking, "How in the world can he blame Mom for his own stupidity?" (I had a precocious love for big words, like "stupidity," normally too large a word for my age.) I determined right then and there never to blame another for my own mistakes. I was not quite four years old, but it was then and there that the Lord wrote it into my heart to always look inside my own self rather than blame others.

When I learned to read, Matthew 7:5 leaped off the page at me and still burns in my heart today, "You hypocrite, first take the log out of your own eye, and then you will see clearly to take the speck out of your brother's eye." Later, that became a linchpin of our counseling, never allowing clients to cast blame outside of themselves without first examining their own hearts' culpability.

## PERSISTENCE IS KEY

My sister Martha Jane was born in California, and then we moved back to the Midwest. My father never continued his studies in medicine. He was a gentle, loving man, but I was to learn later his self-defeating habit: He loved to plan new enterprises and became highly enthused when beginning an adventure that supposedly was a great "get-rich-quick" scheme, only to abandon it altogether or somehow sabotage himself. Consequently, my parents made and lost several fortunes.

This flaw of my father's built into me a determination to abide, an inner vow to persist at whatever task was at hand until it was fully accomplished. Later, I had to break that vow lest I stick at something God wanted me to leave, and lest righteousness be of the flesh, compulsive—rather than from the Lord. But it served me well when I had to work five different jobs to stay at Drury University and then work my way through Chicago Theological Seminary. And that determination never to quit at anything supported me well when years later our pioneering efforts in the prophetic and then inner healing resulted in massive persecution and slander.

## A FIREFLY FAILURE

I began kindergarten in Topeka, Kansas. Nothing formative happened there, except I remember that my mother was of the old school and insisted that Hal and I be in bed by eight o'clock—which we resisted mightily! One evening Hal and I found a two-quart jar, punched holes in the lid, and caught dozens of fireflies. Smuggling the jar full of fireflies up to our room, we planned to look at picture books under the covers by its light. But it didn't work. The fireflies did their part, but they couldn't produce enough light for our little scheme. Needless to say, our first rebellious caper resulted in failure. Somehow, that lodged in my memory some kind of sign to my conscience.

## Do You See What I See?

Shortly thereafter we moved to Independence, Kansas, just down the block from the city park, which had a fascinating monkey island right next to the head of our street. We used to watch the monkeys by the hour. One day my parents had a number of visitors in the house when I burst in to announce excitedly, "There's a monkey on our roof!" Knowing my highly imaginative nature, everyone laughed. But I insisted, and just to humor me, they came outside.

Sure enough, there sat a monkey on our chimney! A branch had fallen into the island and the monkey had used it to scale the wall to freedom. That struck a chord in my mind, a bitter root expectancy that I would see things others don't and be laughed at until others could see what I see. That is still happening today—as it happens to every prophet of the Lord.

## Lessons Through Fear, Falling, and Fighting

We moved to Kansas City, Missouri, where I attended Marlborough Grade School. Three events registered deeply during the four years while we were there. My brother and I slept in a second floor sun porch that had three windows on the north and three on the south with six facing east. By then Mom would let us stay up until nine o'clock. On Wednesdays, however, we could listen to "Gangbusters" till half past nine. Each Gangbusters program ended with a description of the ten most wanted criminals (which, in our fevered imaginations, were all loose in our area).

After the program ended, we'd change into our pajamas and head down the hall to brush our teeth, turning off the light to our room on the way out. After we finished in the bathroom, we would run down the hall back to our room, and without turning on the light, do a flying leap from the floor at the door and land on our beds. Neither of us was brave enough to walk in the dark from the light switch to our bed because, of course, a robber might grab us from under the bed! Then we'd lie there terrified, trying to watch all 12 windows at once, sure we'd see a ladder come poking up. Those were the nights when I learned to pray and to make myself rest, trusting God. From that silly weekly experience I built into myself a discipline of controlling my emotions, which has stood me well throughout my life.

One night Mom slipped in and moved the beds, and we landed with a resounding crash on the hardwood floor! I don't know what that taught me, but it surely should have taught me something!

(Today kids watch all kinds of horror stories on TV and don't seem to be as affected as we were; but that time was a more innocent age, and we were young and naive.)

Around that same time, I learned some valuable lessons about empathy, compassion, and reconciliation through experiencing the opposite. In my neighborhood, gangs of kids around eight to twelve years old fought to own the turf of our area. An especially valuable and coveted place was a wooded area across from where we lived. The kids on the next block beyond fought us for control of that wonderful place to play.

My father had opened a Winkler Stoker store downtown and had put a stoker in our house. Central heating had just been installed in many houses, but Winklers boasted the first fully automatic heating system. Each stoker had a large hopper, which could be filled with small grain coal. A worm (a long metal rod shaped like a screw) carried coal in to a retort in the furnace. Whenever the temperature dropped, an automatic signal sent more coal through the worm for a stronger fire. We used tongs to reach in and lift clinkers out of the retort. Every once in a while, we had to scoop the fine pink ash from a receptacle below the retort and carry it out. We learned to do this very carefully because sudden movements could cause fumes of ash to rise and sting our eyes unmercifully and choke our throats until it became hard to breathe.

My brother and I discovered a way of using this unpleasant attribute of the ash to our advantage. Wrapping the ash in tissue paper, we made pink ash grenades that exploded on or in front of our enemies with torturous effect. Furious gang members then chased us out of the woods and right into a trap we had set! A mattress box had been placed between bushes at the street edge of our yard with only some eye holes and a space cut for a protruding hose nozzle. Knowing that our house enjoyed extremely strong water pressure, my brother and some of our friends ran behind the box and, at just the right moment, yelled for me to turn on the hose—which I did. Now the ash that clung to our opponents' clothes became mud, and they were doused from head to toe. They looked and felt a miserable mess, and they dared not charge at the hose or onto the lawn for fear of deadly aimed ash missiles. However, they soon learned that I was unguarded and exposed at the faucet and all of them began to hurl rocks at me. I found it little problem to dodge the rocks but was greatly gratified when they finally gave up and went home.

I remember to this day how I felt when it was over. Although victory was complete, I felt totally ambivalent! Though on one hand I was able to rejoice with my brother and our friends, on the other hand I felt sick at heart at the other gang's disgrace. The hang dog look of shame on their faces hurt my heart, even though I was only about nine years old and did not yet know the Lord.

Later we made peace with that gang and played a lot of sandlot football with them. They became our best friends. But something was written deeply in my heart during those puerile wars. The gift of burden bearing was already keenly at work—though I didn't understand it then. I just knew their pain was my pain. I felt their disgrace and shame all the way through me. I found in those experiences that it hurt my heart too much to inflict pain on others. Victory wasn't worth the price. I would still fight to win if pushed (and have never lost a fight), but I never enjoyed it and never again initiated fighting. Reconciliation became important to me even at that feisty age of nine.

## SENSING TROUBLE BREWING

My father was a poor judge of character. His kindness, coupled with greed to make a dollar, blinded him from seeing that a man in his employ was untrustworthy. From what I can tell, my mother, who had a keen sense of discernment, had been warning Dad about this employee, but he wasn't listening. Mom was disgusted, and though they hid all arguments and problems from us, I sensed something was wrong.

I remember as though it were yesterday how on Christmas morning in 1939 I felt prompted in my spirit to look into the garage. There sat a new 1939 black Ford sedan, a Christmas gift from Dad to Mom. I guess I should have been rejoicing that the family would have a nice car to ride in, but I couldn't. I knew in my spirit that something was wrong. I was too young then to know what. Later I came to understand that while on the surface this was a gift and a peace offering, covertly Dad was trying to buy off my mother's hurts and suspicions.

Mom knew trouble was coming and used her Osage allotment (which she received because of her Native American descent) to put money down on a house in the country, west of Mission, Kansas, a few miles west of the Missouri-Kansas border. She figured that if Dad lost his business, we could plant a large garden, raise milk cows and chickens, and survive. When I was in the sixth grade in 1940, we moved next door to Shawnee Mission High School, into the only house still standing just east of what is now Shawnee Mission North High School. We soon had two milk cows, three hundred chickens, a 38-tree orchard, and more than a half acre of garden.

## FEAR IS FAST

Hickory Grove Grade School was about half a mile south of our house, across a dairy farmer's pasture. Going around the pasture meant going about a quarter mile further, so of course we cut across, despite the farmer's protests that we'd upset his cattle and make them run. Whenever his big old bull chased us, we got away by leaping off a high bank across a stream.

In our class at school was a boy named Bobby Bodine, about as chunky as his name sounds. He couldn't run fast, so he was always the last to be selected for school yard games. One day I invited him to go home with me after school. We were about halfway through the pasture when along came the farmer, standing in the back of his pickup with a shotgun while his driver took off across the pasture after us. I was one of the faster runners in the class, but Bobby Bodine passed me like I was standing still! I found him sitting outside the fence by the highway, waiting for me. I was amazed, but that certainly taught me what fear could do! And I never forgot it.

### EXPERIENCES IN WAR TIMES

On Sunday, December 7, 1941, our family happened not to turn on the radio that day. The next day, as I entered my seventh grade class, I felt a pall over the room so thick you could almost cut it with a knife. That was when I found out what had happened, and our classes listened to the radio that day as America responded and our country went to war.

The government soon subsidized Winkler stokers in order to save fuel. The man my mother had distrusted said he sold many stokers. But, in actuality, he made up fictitious names, hid the stokers in a warehouse, and pocketed the money from the government. He got away with it until he failed to make a few payments, and the government found him out. My father was indicted along with him. Eventually Dad was cleared, but paying off the lawyers took all our money. Since the man had been in my father's employ, the government decreed that my father had to pay back all the embezzled money. Actually, they had expected my father to file bankruptcy and simply charged him because they had to blame someone. However, Dad felt responsible and went to work in two war plants, 16 hours a day, turning in every paycheck to return all the money. We survived on what I could raise in the garden and with the cows and chickens and my mother's Osage allotment.

My mother was Osage allottee number 2229, the next to the last of the Osages. The Osage Indian rolls had been closed on June 15, 1907. My mother was born that year, June 9th. Wise counselors in the tribe had decreed that any Osage could sell his 770 acres of allotted land, but whatever would be found in the ground below or the air above would belong to the whole tribe, no matter who owned the land. One of history's richest oil fields was discovered in Osage County, Oklahoma, and every enrolled member of the tribe became wealthy overnight. But the Osages were still Stone Age people. Pioneers had tramped west over their land in Kansas, not bothering then to stop and settle, and the Osages had remained a pocket of isolated, undeveloped, uncivilized people. They knew nothing about money. Unscrupulous white men came in to try to swindle the Osages. Our country's Federal Bureau of Investigation, which became famous under the abbreviation "FBI," was formed initially to investigate the swindling of the Osages!

Early on, each headright yielded thousands of dollars every quarter. Those were the fortunes my parents managed to lose, several times. But at this time in our lives, the yields were down to only about three hundred dollars every quarter, which was what we survived on, along with what I could raise.

Those were the years in which parental inversion gripped my life. My older brother was into teenage rebellion and then later was drafted into the army. My father was gone all day long, six days a week. My younger sister was too young to be much help, and by then a baby brother also had to be cared for. Under all that stress, my mother became a hypochondriac. I used to say it took a strong woman to get that sick. To my angry mind, it seemed that if there was work to do, she became deathly ill and took to her bed. But if there was a party to attend, she had a miraculous healing! So, after initially working alongside me, she petered out, and all the work fell to me.

My mother had the "you call a spade a spade" mentality, and when Hal began to drink and run with wild women, she clamped down, which only drove him further into trouble. Hal reacted with more anger and rebellion. At last, he went to live with Aunt Tresia, mother's younger sister, during his senior year, and turned around to become an upstanding citizen. Before that, I remember riding beside my father late at night while he drove the streets and wept, trying to find Hal and bring him home. So, I was my father's counselor and my mother's confidant, and because Dad was gone so much, the father to my sister and younger brother.

## A Lesson About Loyalty and Love

After he was drafted, Hal didn't want to come home on leave. Because he was still angry at Mom and Dad, he didn't want to see them; on the other hand he wanted to see me. Late one night he phoned. I thought I had picked up the phone before Dad and Mom heard it and didn't realize that Dad was listening in on the last part of the conversation on the upstairs phone. Hal wanted me to dress, slip out, and meet him at a local all-night café. Dad had only heard part of the conversation so he didn't know where Hal was. He came down and found me quietly dressing—and put me in the most painful place I had ever been in.

If I gave in and told Dad where Hal was, I felt I would betray Hal's trust. But if I didn't tell Dad, Mom and he would be equally wounded and feel just as betrayed. I knew Dad wouldn't force me, and he didn't. He remained kind and patient—which hurt all the more. Finally, I decided to hope for reconciliation, and my father and I went to see Hal.

That night Hal came home. He and my parents talked out their differences and forgave one another. But I felt guilty. It hurt that I felt I had to betray my brother's trust, yet on the other hand it shamed me to sneak out when I knew my parents wanted to see their eldest son.

I learned from that experience that loving people can exact a high price—and I resolved to pay it. Being a mediator can call for laying down one's life, as it did for Jesus. Among other things, my pride of loyalty had to die that night for the sake of possible reconciliation. I learned from my father's example not to force obedience.

My father also taught me to pay the price of suffering and prayer for those we love as I rode beside him in the long futile nights of searching for a prodigal son and brother.

My mother's outraged insistence, Hal's rebellious reaction, my father's sufferings and patience, the eventual outcome, and the story of the prodigal in Luke 15 coalesced in my heart and mind to become one of the foundation stones of inner healing. From those experiences and relationships, I resolved never to impose a methodology of healing on anyone, but to pay the price of burden bearing and patience in faith so that others can be healed by the Lord in His own time and way—and so that others gain the wisdom God intends. I saw my brother become a strong moral man and knew he had acquired wisdom that perhaps he could have gained no other way than through all he experienced.

## MY TEENAGE YEARS

I didn't have to personally survive the struggles of teenage rebelliousness; I lived it vicariously through my brother. I thought, *That's dumb*, and determined never to hurt my parents as I saw Hal and other teenagers hurting theirs. (That didn't mean I was a teenage saint. I had my own list of sins that showed me later on my need of a Savior.) But I did understand teenage struggles, and that knowledge, which was gained from painful experience, became part of the wisdom in giving counsel to thousands of parents later on.

Having to work so much gave me little opportunity to make friends. There was simply no time. One of the few friends I did have was a bad influence. He lived close by, and I figured that a friend like him was better than no friends at all. Unfortunately, he introduced me to pornography and inappropriate sexual desires—lust.

A funny thing happened that began to shock me clear of that lust. Next door to our house, on the east side, was a family who had a well-built older teenage daughter. Her bedroom window opened out toward our lawn, and she never bothered to draw the shades. I was so myopic, even with glasses, that I could have seen little anyway, but the prospect was thrilling! In order to achieve the best viewing angle, when she would walk south, I would walk north. Then I found I could get out onto our flat porch roof and see even better. One night she walked too far north and I walked too far south—right off the roof 15 feet to the ground! I lay there a bit stunned, checking limbs one by one, and found I wasn't hurt at all. However, that episode taught my lustful heart some valuable lessons! I immediately began to fight clear of lust and found great relief years later when inner healing cleansed my heart of the memories of those wrongful emotions and corresponding guilt.

During that time I had another friend named Roger Wagner, a fine young teenager whose heart and mind were clean. He listened to my mystical imaginative stories and thoughts with compassion, even if he didn't understand sometimes. I've always been grateful for his friendship during those troubled years of war in the world and tensions in my home.

Through these two friends the Lord wrote onto my heart the truth of two Scriptures I've never forgotten. "Bad company corrupts good morals" (1 Cor. 15:33b). And "He who walks with wise men will be wise, but the companion of fools will suffer harm" (Prov. 13:20).

At last, at the end of my sophomore year, the war ended, and a year later we moved back to Joplin, Missouri, where I had been born.

## CHAPTER THREE

# PAULA'S FOUNDATION FOR AN EARLY CALL

Today we find ourselves living in a world that poses numerous threats: natural disasters, political upheaval, terrorist attacks, and all manner of wars. Some people are living in denial, pretending that everything is fine; some are struggling with great anxiety and even panic when biological warfare or nuclear weapons are mentioned. More and more people are afraid to fly. Even many of those who call themselves Christian are having a difficult time casting their cares on the Lord, especially when they have lost their jobs and credit debts overwhelm them. More and more often, people are allowing fear to rise up and erupt in uncontrolled anger, which is very destructive.

Too many people in our American culture have learned to depend on material things for security. And too few have known or experienced the kind of family life that builds a solid foundation, which enables trust in God. I thank the Lord that my parents laid a good foundation for me, my three brothers, and sister.

My parents were devout Christians and I'm sure they carried in their hearts the essence and blessing of the prayer in Psalm 57:1 (NKJV): "Be merciful to me, O God, be merciful to me! For my soul trusts in You; and in the shadow of Your wings I will make my refuge, until these calamities have passed by."

### IN THE MIDST OF CALAMITIES

I was born in the midst of calamities. Very soon after my parents were married, my mother's appendix burst, peritonitis set in, and she nearly died. When she was released from the hospital some time later, doctors told her she should absolutely not get pregnant for at least a year. However, warning notwithstanding, I was conceived very shortly after that.

It never entered my mother's mind to have an abortion, but emotionally she was torn between love of her baby-to-come and abject fear all during the pregnancy that she might split open as I grew. Delivery was difficult for her, and to add to her worries, I was born with an enlarged thymus, which doctors then treated with X rays.

Otherwise I was a healthy redhead, but I cried all the time. My mother tried to comfort me by holding and rocking me and softly singing, talking to me, and praying; but I couldn't be comforted. A near neighbor, a nurse, tried to help, but I cried all the more.

At that time, my father's job as a salesman for General Foods Company required that he travel during the week. Since jobs were scarce in 1931, he really had no alternative. The moment he would arrive home from each trip and take me into his arms I would settle peacefully, and the moment he left I would resume my crying. Even my uncle Henry's efforts to console me failed.

Looking back, I believe I was probably experiencing my mother's feelings as well as my own feelings concerning my daddy's absence. We now recognize that situation as being a lesson of burden bearing with a degree of spiritual sensitivity the Lord gives us from the beginning of our lives. In addition, we now know that I felt like an unwanted intrusion and a danger to my mother because of her condition and her ambivalent feelings—so I cried all the time; and only my dad, who wanted me very much, could comfort me.

## Lessons From Heat, Dust, and a Weekend Dad

My brother Jerry was born within the next three years and my brother Stan 20 months after him. My earliest memories were of the intensely hot Kansas summers in Dodge City and windstorms that blew great clouds of dust across the land. Many times my father wore a mask over his face to filter the dust when he was on the road.

One day (before there was air conditioning) a large stack of advertising materials in the back of his panel truck ignited from the heat and he could do nothing but stand on the prairie and watch his truck burn. I don't know how he got home that evening, but I do know that we could depend on his arriving home every weekend with hugs for his family. His joyful greetings and faithfulness to lovingly care for and reassure us built into me a basic trust of Father God and an expectation that He would do the same for me as my father had, only better.

There was a time in my adult life when I had to deal both with my picture of a weekend father and consequently a Father God who was permitted by my faulty heart's bitter root expectancies to show up only on the weekends. I never felt anger toward my father because I knew he was traveling to earn for us the things we needed. Choosing to forgive him for not having been close when I needed him on weekdays opened my heart to receive touches of my heavenly Father whenever and wherever I reach out to Him—or He to me. Father God is not only in my church on the weekends, but is always present in my life, often reaching out to me.

When storm warnings came on the radio we would roll up the living room rug and carefully tape around our windows and doors. Mother would cover the beds with sheets to protect them from dust, and we would sleep on the floor all night with wet washcloths across our faces. In the morning we could see our silhouettes outlined in the dust on the floor despite our preparations. The discomfort caused by heat and dust was always delightfully alleviated when mother would place a washtub full of water in the backyard by the hose with which we laughingly sprayed one another. Although we enjoyed cleaning the dust off ourselves, I doubt that Mom had much fun as she hung the rug across the clothesline to beat out the dust with a broom; but I remember enjoying it when she'd let me "help" her.

From these things I learned from both my parents that we can choose to make the most of difficult situations. The only things I really liked about Dodge City were the thousands of giant sunflowers and the abundance of jackrabbits. Although we children loved to watch the rabbits, the state declared a bounty on them because they were such a menace on the highways.

## What Playing With My Father Taught Me

When I was two my daddy taught me to roller-skate. The metal skates we had then were adjustable to any size and fit over our shoes. Daddy would wear one skate and I the other, and we held hands as we skated down the sidewalk. It was also a lot of fun to pull my brother Jerry along in his little red wagon.

Because my father always took time after a week of hard work to enjoy being with his children, I knew that Father God, busy as He is with His universe, would still take time out for me. It was easy to believe in a loving heavenly Father.

The Bible says that when Jesus became weary from teaching and ministering to the multitudes all day, the disciples tried to keep the children away from Him. But Jesus told His disciples to let the children come to Him, "for the kingdom of heaven belongs to such as these" (Mt. 19:14b). The Scripture then says that He touched them and departed from there. Our son Mark, who loves to study the Greek meanings of words, tells us that the word used here for "touch" indicates a loving and lingering embrace. This means that Jesus took time to truly bless the children before He departed. (Perhaps the disciples knew that though Jesus planned to leave, He would give the children much more than the usual pat on the head given by a rabbi, so they tried to send the children away in order to allow time for more teaching.) My parents would often take time from important tasks they were involved in to pay attention to our needs; their attention built within me an ability to believe in the Lord's desire to meet us, know us, and sacrifice for us.

## Lessons During the Great Depression

In 1929, before I was born, the stock market crashed and the Great Depression followed. During my childhood thousands of people were out of work, and we heard about many who committed suicide following loss of fortunes. Our family fortune was never lost because it couldn't be counted in monetary terms.

My father always had a job, but his paycheck was barely enough to cover basic expenses. He made toys for us and played with us when he was home. He always found some way to make us laugh. Mother skillfully made attractive play clothes from colorfully print-ed flour sacks, and sometimes made our underwear from still-sturdy cloth from the corners of old sheets. We ate simply but healthily, and Mother was always glad to fix a small bag of sandwiches to give to the many beggars who came to our door. We learned that sharing what you have is an important part of living. We learned that God supplies, and that we really can't outgive Him. (After I married John and our finances often became scarce, I didn't really fear because I knew what God could do.)

Mother read many good stories to us, and a great number of them came from the Bible. We had prayer at meals and bedtime. We went to church regularly, but I have only one vivid memory of Sun-day school when I was small. I was very unhappy with the teacher. I remember sitting up high in a windowsill, resisting whatever was happening and wishing I were somewhere else. I told my parents I didn't want to go there anymore because I didn't like being treated like a baby. I still don't remember what followed—only that my par-ents listened and seemed to understand. I believe that incident placed a seed of expectation that Father God would also listen with understanding.

I was glad when we moved to Wichita for a short time, and then to West Plains, Missouri, where I entered first grade at the age of five and was soon placed in the second grade reading class. I credit my mother's inspiration for my rapid advancement. Listening to her read stories built within us an appetite for reading.

Daddy occasionally brought us candy—or at least that's what we called it. It was really fruit gelatin that had dried and hardened. It was no longer fit for sale but how we loved it! Mother would also sometimes help us mix and pull molasses taffy—what fun in the kitchen! Occasionally we were blessed with special treats when Dad would take us riding and give us each a nickel to spend—back when a nickel was worth something!

IMAGINATION, FUN IN THE NEIGHBORHOOD,
AND LEARNING TO TAKE RISKS

When Dad went to work for Faultless Starch Company, we moved to St. Louis, Missouri. It was August, hot and humid, and we stayed a month or so with my grandparents in a fourplex until we could find a place of our own. There was no air conditioning in those days, so the whole neighborhood would take their bedding to Tower Grove Park at night to get some sleep. What an adventure that was—a cross-generational slumber party! No one would dare to do that today—at least not in that location! We then moved to southwest St. Louis as soon as we found a house for rent. Our wealth multiplied in relationship with one another and with new friends in our neighborhood and church as we shared together. My brother Lee and my sister Sue were born there.

There were lots of fun things we did to occupy ourselves. We lived on a hill, and I found the sidewalk to be a wonderful challenge on roller skates. The fun I had made risk-taking worthwhile despite occasionally skinned knees. Later I learned to stand on the seat of a used bicycle, pretending I was in the circus. Almost every evening all the kids in the neighborhood gathered in the street to jump rope or play games such as hide-and-seek or red rover. In spring and summer we picked large red clover blossoms and wove them together. At night we caught lightning bugs and put them in jars. Sometimes we caught tadpoles in a nearby pond, or slid down the hill in the park on "sleds" we made from cardboard boxes. What a wonderful gift of imagination and creativity God has given to children!

(The flip side of the wonderful benefits we have today in prosperous America is that our children are too much and too often deprived of the wondrous gift of making fun out of nothing as we had to do. Along came TV, and everyone became watchers!)

I experienced a short-lived problem with a first grade teacher who called me "stupid" because I wouldn't write my name on the blackboard "properly." She insisted I was "Pauline" and I had to stand my ground to convince her I was "Paula." Actually my argument with the teacher was good for me because I learned to stand up for myself despite my shyness.

Second grade went fine. I reigned as the "handwriting queen" because I had already learned cursive writing in my West Plains school. I was given a double promotion and skipped the last half of third grade. John calls that a "God thing" because if I had arrived at Drury a half year later he would have become too serious with Alice (his girlfriend at that time) to become interested in me.

### THE GOOD EFFECTS OF FAMILY SINGING AND A WHOLESOME CHURCH FAMILY

In our home we enjoyed singing around the piano in the evening. Mother played the piano and Dad his clarinet. Listening to good music and playing games were blessings that have lasted to this day. I managed to read at least three library books a week and selections from *The Book of Knowledge*. I also drew pictures on every piece of paper I could find.

We drove 15 miles to church every Sunday to worship at Third Baptist Church in downtown St. Louis. It was a mega-church of 6500 members—2500 in Sunday school classes in a day—at a time when mega-churches were hardly existent. I loved singing in the children's choir. I felt at home in my church and listened to the pastor's sermons with rapt attention.

The church was unusual in that it was Northern (American) Baptist in the morning and Southern Baptist in the evening. The senior pastor, Dr. C. Oscar Johnson, believed in unity among the churches, as Jesus so passionately prayed for in John 17:21: "That they all may be one, as You, Father, are in Me, and I in You; that they also may be one in Us, that the world may believe that You sent Me."

Dr. Johnson was the president of both Baptist conferences at different times, and he was once president of the Baptist World Alliance. St. Louis University (a Catholic institution) was just down the street, and he offered them the use of our church to provide them with much-needed classroom space during the week. Dr. Johnson welcomed the children of the neighborhood into the gymnasium to skate during the week. There was food, clothing, and other items available for the needy, and instruction provided to them if they needed to be taught how to use what was given. His attitude and actions built beliefs and practices into me that prepared me for ministry in many denominations years later.

Dr. Johnson was always warm and friendly. He never criticized others, and he preached a powerful gospel message that emphasized the birth, life, death, and resurrection of Jesus Christ and what His sacrifice accomplished for us. Every Sunday I was more and more convinced that Jesus died for me and that He was calling me to make a commitment of my life to Him.

When I was 11 years old, Dr. Johnson gave the invitation for people to come forward to dedicate their lives to Jesus. I had to do it! Disregarding my shyness, and without saying a word to my parents, I stood up and walked by myself down a very long aisle to the front of the church to shake my pastor's hand and confess my faith in Jesus Christ as my Savior and Lord. I believe my parents were startled but rejoicing. I talked with a deaconess, went the next week to talk with members of the Diaconate, and then was baptized by immersion. It was a marvelous experience!

The first time I participated in a communion service I was completely bathed in the Presence of the Lord. Tears welled up from deep inside of me—an emotion that poured forth each time communion was served from then on. My parents were a bit concerned that such a thing would bring tears to my eyes; but communion always affected me that way, despite the fact that it was always referred to as only a *remembrance* of Christ. I remembered all right, but at the same time felt that He had come to sit with us at His table.

My parents also didn't really seem to understand why I would become teary each time I saw other people coming forward. I didn't try to explain. I tried to control my emotions, but always deep inside I knew the Lord was calling me for something special. Later on, I was a bit disturbed when I discovered that my continual attempts to control my emotions had built into me such a strong practice of control that my emotions were blocked far too much, especially in relating freely to God's Presence. Finally, I asked the Lord to set me free emotionally and He answered my prayers.

## LEARNING TO SERVE DESPITE STRONG EMOTIONS

When I was barely 14, I was asked to teach a regular class of children in the Primary Department at the church, and then to fill in for the Primary Department Superintendent for the summer months. I loved it and felt at home. Some time later, a little boy in my class was killed when he tried to skate holding onto the back of a pickup truck. His parents asked me to sing a song about little children who know their Redeemer. I thought I couldn't possibly do so without falling apart emotionally, but I was assured that I could sing from behind the curtain. I prayed that the Lord would take charge and sing through me, and He did. I began to get the idea that if God calls me to do something, it isn't so important that I know how to get something done; more importantly is that I let Jesus do through me whatever it is He calls me to do. That early lesson has stood me well over the years as John and I have been catapulted into prominence and awesome responsibilities and situations.

## STIRRINGS, BUT FOR WHAT?

I had not heard much about the Holy Spirit in my church, but neither had I ever heard a word against the reality of the Holy Spirit and His gifts. This was a tremendous blessing because I had nothing to unlearn years later when the Holy Spirit began to fall on John and me. Beginning in my early teen years, I had felt that I was being called to some kind of missions work. I even studied Spanish in high school, thinking that some day I might need to use that language. I knew I was called; however, I didn't know yet to what.

When I was 16 I worked all summer as a nurse's aide at Missouri Baptist Hospital. I bathed patients, made beds, carried food, and combed patients' hair; and every day I gave back rubs to each one assigned to me. On a number of occasions I remember patients asking me, "Are you a healer? Your hands are so warm!" I had never heard of "healers," but I did tell them I was sure that Jesus heals. Little did

I know that some day I would be praying for many people with "laying on of hands" for healing of all kinds of illnesses, from the physical to emotional to spiritual.

Some of the hospital staff encouraged me to study nursing, but I didn't feel a call to go in that direction. So, after graduating from high school in January 1949, I continued teaching my Sunday school class while working in disbursement accounting for the telephone company. By the fall of that year I had accumulated enough money to enroll at Drury University in Springfield, Missouri.

### INTIMATIONS...

Not long ago, on May 5, 2002, I suddenly remembered the words of a poem I composed while I was still working in the hospital:

> I may be a bell in the steeple
> and sing to the land in a voice great and loud.
> Or I may be a stone both trampled and scorned
> 'neath the feet of the worshiping crowd.
> Whatever my job is destined to be,
> no matter how great or how small,
> I want to be able to say when I'm through
> that I've given my best, my all.

Today I recognize the prophetic quality of those words, and thank God for His unfailing, empowering love through the years for bells and stones like me.

CHAPTER FOUR

# John's High School and College Years

H alfway through my junior year at Shawnee Mission High School, my parents bought a great old house at 619 Sergeant, Joplin, Missouri. I went to Joplin immediately to take care of the house and prepare for the family to move there during the summer.

By then, oil companies had devised a method of pumping salt water into oil wells that would cause the oil to float up. This development increased Osage royalties again to thousands of dollars each quarter. My mother had also begun to receive inheritance money from the death of her father, who had owned a 5,270-acre cattle ranch and several other smaller properties. With her share amongst seven inheritors (her mother, four brothers, and one sister), she purchased this fine house—which, by the way, has been preserved as a national historical landmark and can be seen on tour in Joplin to this day.

In addition, my father purchased the Joplin area franchise for Sartol, a company that produced fine healing salves and ointments and a drink that was supposed to heal everything from sore throats to bunions. He thought it would grow into a major business, with many route salesmen, serving grocery stores and pharmacies throughout the area. But eventually, along with its failure came another loss of fortune.

Meanwhile, the cows and chickens had been sold. The garden and the fruit trees were a thing of the past, and for the first time I had the opportunity to have a normal high school life. I joined the Latin Club and several other groups, went out for track, and spent a lot of time at the YMCA, which was still for men only in those days and very Christian. I was no longer a fast runner but had staying power, so I ran the mile. My friend Rod Meredith and I lifted weights at the YMCA and ran the mile together. We came in first and second at every race except one. He was always first and I always second.

## First Encounter With the Gospel Message

At the end of my junior year came an event that changed my life. My family attended the First Community Church of Joplin, right next to the YMCA—another good but liberal church. A lively youth fellowship met at the church, and though its leaders didn't know the gospel, they made sure we were busily involved in wholesome activities that kept us out of trouble.

For some reason one day I volunteered to go to the First Christian Church, one block north of our church—I forget why—maybe to borrow something. There, in a meeting on the second floor, was a beautiful blonde girl from my junior class, Jodie Klarquist, a full-blood Swede. There was an instant mutual attraction. We dated steadily from that time through our senior year. We thought we were in love, but during the summer after our senior year we each left to attend separate universities and eventually married different partners. But because I attended church with her many times, I heard for the first time a life-changing message—the gospel.

Preacher Brown preached a simple heart-touching message on the Sunday and Wednesday evenings I attended church with Jodie. These began to infiltrate my heart. I was still too imbued with liberalism to accept wholeheartedly his simple, down-to-earth biblical messages, which seemed too narrow and unsophisticated for my "magnanimous philosophical mind." But the Word of God sank in and began to spread its roots deeper and deeper into my heart. The pastor's wife, Blossom Brown, whose name hit me as so typical of backwoods Ozarkian mentality, nevertheless greatly impacted me with her gentle, loving heart.

## Following God's Laws of Purity

Jodie and I shared some passionate times together. But in those days, even liberals were taught that the Ten Commandments were absolutely law. The foolishness of relativity had not yet undone belief and reverence for the eternal revelation and relevance of the laws of God.

*Thy word I have treasured in my heart, that I may not sin against Thee* (Psalm 119:11).

*Moreover, by them [the commandments of God] Thy servant is warned; in keeping them there is great reward* (Psalm 19:11).

Whenever Jodie and I would get physical and want to go too far, I can remember as though it were yesterday how the Lord would take His commandments and rush them into my consciousness, fogging down my flames like a fire extinguisher! "Thou shalt not commit adultery." "Do not rob a brother of his glory." Then I'd also remember my mother's teachings to keep myself pure to the wife I'd marry someday, and statements like, "You don't know whose glory a girl will be, maybe not yours."

These things would ricochet through my mind and heart, and I just couldn't go any further. Remember, so many years earlier, I had made that inner vow never to hurt another human being. I knew that within every woman is a glory meant only for her husband. So we never went all the way, nor even did much beyond simple kissing. (The same proved true with Alice, whom I dated before Paula came to the university.)

I have never known any woman sexually other than my wife, Paula, and I can never adequately tell anyone how grateful I am that God has kept me only to her all these years! I grieve for today's youth who, for the most part, do not have the protection our generation knew. Nor do they know that there is a glory God has created between husbands and wives that can be found only there, which is destroyed by promiscuity.

## OTHER FAMILY BUSINESSES

When the Sartol business failed, my father discovered that the big laundry soap companies had not yet come back into full production after the war. He knew he could get every ingredient he needed to produce soap, including renderings of lard from a local butchering house. So he found an expert who set up a soap factory and Dad went out to sell. Hal and I worked hour after hour making laundry soap. Dad hoped to be so established with a line of satisfied customers that by the time the larger soap companies returned, we would be well on our way to a continually profitable business. But...that didn't work either. Those laundry soap producers soon undercut our costs of production, and that business of Dad's folded also.

Because my mother was an expert knitter, also skilled in pettipoint and other needlework, crocheting, tatting, and embroidery, she and Dad opened a yarn and thread shop where women would come to visit and knit and buy materials. On the other side of our store space we sold many gifts and even a smattering of very fine furniture. I worked in the warehouse and on the delivery truck of the big Joplin Furniture Company in order to earn money for college and also helped out in our family store on weekends.

### CALLED TO MINISTER

In the spring of 1947 as I was spading a plot of ground at the back of our lawn for a small garden, the clouds moved and the sun shone through in the form of a cross. As I looked at that formation, the Lord spoke very clearly, "You are to be a minister." Years later I realized I never thought it surprising or strange that God spoke to me. It had not been an audible voice, but it was so powerful within my mind that I never questioned that I had heard God. God had spoken, and that was it.

That fall I preached my first sermon before going off to the university. The same afternoon my mother sat me down and told me the story of her dream and my birth. She said that she had waited, wanting my call to come to me from God, rather than from her dream. Now that His call had come and I had responded, she felt I should know.

That catapulted me into a frantic search to find out what I was supposed to do. Or rather, I hurled myself. What she told me rang bells all throughout my system. I knew then why I had always possessed such a mystical bent, and why I had withdrawn so often into the attic to read about the prophets in the Bible and ponder. It explained why I had sought to be in church all my life and after moving to Joplin found my friends there. It told me why I reacted so strongly in hurt and disappointment whenever Christians' behavior did not measure up to the standard of Jesus' life. I did not yet know that He was the very Son of God our Savior, but the liberal church had taught me well that He is our model and standard for all our actions. I loved God and it had puzzled me why it hurt me so much for Him when His people disgraced His name. Now I know those senses come as part of the birthright and equipment of the Lord's prophets. But all of those desires and reactions had remained as unanswered questions until that afternoon.

The revelation of my mother's dream told me why I seemed imbued with such a conscience. I never could run with the wild guys in my school. I knew that most hormone-driven teenagers plunged right on into sex, even in those more moral days, and in the locker room I had overheard some of the "jocks" bragging about their sexual exploits. I had wondered why that hurt me so much, and why God had kept me so virginal though I had been sorely tempted.

Having been raised in the liberal church, I hadn't searched for truth, whereas I would begin now. In fact, I went on a frantic quest, without knowing our Lord Jesus Christ *is* the Truth. My search consisted of two main questions: (1) Where was the power that was exhibited in the early Church? Where were the signs and wonders that vindicated the disciples and made their testimony so powerful as to convert the Roman Empire within three hundred years? (2) Who was truly and fully living the lifestyle of love and self-sacrifice that Jesus lived for 33 years among us? It was this latter question that drove me into the discoveries of knowledge that became the foundation of inner healing.

In those days no one but a few "Holy Rollers" knew anything about the Holy Spirit. The Assemblies of God, the Four Square Church, and various other Pentecostals knew the power of the Holy

Spirit and were beginning to explode evangelistically around the world, but none of the "old-line churches" had any awareness except to scoff at what we considered to be emotional excesses.

So I sought answers in all the wrong places. I read voraciously about several other religions—Hinduism, Mohammedanism, Buddhism, and every other "ism." I poured over many philosophical works—Socrates, Plato, Aristotle, Hegel, Kant, and Schleiermacher, then all the enlightenment authors such as Rousseau and Descartes, followed by the existentialists such as Kierkegaard. I studied every kind of mysticism I heard of—American Indian mysticism, especially Osage, the German mystics such as Meister Eckhart, American pietism, and on into occult studies of Edgar Cayce, Gina Cerminara the reincarnationist, Rosicrucianism, theosophists such as Madame Blavatsky, etc., ad nauseum. Mind you, I didn't do that studying all at once; this fevered searching went on for many years, starting that afternoon with my mother and continuing throughout my time at the university and most of my seminary training.

At one point, my parents saw what was happening and called me home from Drury University. "Jackie," Dad said (that was still my nickname in those days), "don't you think if God was able to give your mother that dream so many years ago, and then in His own time and way, call you into His service, He is also able to reveal to you what you need to know without all this frantic searching?"

That was good sound advice. But I couldn't receive it. "They just don't know the weight on my shoulders. I've got to find out the answers!" Though I was carrying a full load scholastically, and working my way through the university with five different jobs, I went on spending every spare moment for which I could muster up enough energy to search here and there and everywhere.

## ON TO SCHOOL...

In the fall of 1947 after I preached my first sermon, it was time for Jodie to go one way and I the other. As I mentioned, I went off to Drury University, in Springfield, Missouri, a Congregational liberal arts school about 75 miles from Joplin. Jodie went to a Bible college in California where she met and eventually married Vernon Rodgers, a fine young ministerial student.

In those days the leaders in the Congregational denomination advised young people not to go directly to a Bible college or seminary, but to get as broad an education as possible in a university, and then after those four years to go on to a theological seminary. They suggested that we not take many religious or Bible courses at the university but that we should expand our minds through economics, psychology, philosophy, literature, and science so that we would be able to minister to people educated in every other field. We could concentrate on the Bible and religious matters later on in seminary.

Though liberalism failed in many ways, that bit of counsel proved to be wise. Years later I found that many of my colleagues, trained in Bible colleges and nothing else, were indeed well equipped biblically, but lacked a broad base of knowledge that could have helped them relate more relevantly to their parishioners.

I majored in English Literature and minored in Sociology. Hungry for anything mystical, I especially devoured Wordsworth, Keats, Byron, and Shakespeare. Smatterings of mysticality could be found throughout their writings.

But the most influential person in all my life to that point became Rabbi Ernst Jacob, who had fled with his wife, Joanna, from Nazi Germany. Both became professors at Drury University. He had an encyclopedic mind and a gentle loving spirit. With him I studied English history, European history, second and third-year German, Old Testament history, and a course on the Old Testament prophets. I loved him and became an assistant to him and his wife in the German department—she taught first-year German—and I graded hundreds of papers of their first and second-year students. Though I had to disregard many things I learned later on in seminary, which I considered to be heretical or just plain old rubbish, I never had to throw away anything Rabbi Jacob taught me! In fact, most of the background of understanding later on in my prophetic experiences and what I wrote in *The Elijah Task* and later in *Elijah Among Us* concerning Old

Testament prophets came from class notes in courses with Rabbi Jacob.

From my personal contact with a rabbi and the lessons he taught me came a great love for the Hebrew people and part of my passion for reconciliation between Christians and Jews. If Ernst and Joanna did not recognize Jesus as the Messiah they had waited for so long as they passed from this life into the hereafter and are not waiting for me there, I am going to be sorely disappointed.

Allow me a bit of a digression from my own story. One of the saddest and most ironic events I've never been able to understand was the circumstances of their deaths. After Ernst and Joanna retired from Drury, they purchased an apartment in which their bedroom was located above a shared garage. One night as someone left a car running in the garage, carbon monoxide gas seeped upwards into their room. This lovely couple who had fled from Nazi Germany in order not to be gassed in Hitler's execution chambers were gassed to death in their own beds! Strange! And strange to me that I'm fighting tears still today as I write about it.

## What I Learned Outside the Classroom

During most of that first year at Drury and the second, I went steady with a lovely German girl, Alice Hintz. I thought I loved her and came close to proposing marriage, but God had other and better plans.

In the first year, I managed to scrape up enough money to join the Lambda Chi Fraternity. I didn't have the time or the money to live in the frat house or socialize with the brothers, but I became the pledge instructor and enjoyed the meetings. This was immediately after the Second World War and many of the students were hardened veterans, catching up on the years they had missed. Rubbing shoulders with those rough men was good for me. It didn't take them long to catch on to my righteous nature and so they took it upon themselves to tease me out of self-righteousness. I remember how in one meeting they were teasing me about all my alleged sexual affairs and how one night I had supposedly been in bed with a girl. I cried out indignantly, "I did not! I was in bed by nine-thirty." Then one wag called out, "Yeah. And by midnight he got up and went home." The meeting erupted in laughter, and I did too. I learned among those ex-soldiers not to take myself too seriously.

## WHAT HUMOR WROTE ON MY HEART

Stone Chapel was a beautiful, old, white stone building in which compulsory religious services were held at 10:00 a.m. every Tuesday morning. Many of the students hated that attendance was mandatory, especially some of the veterans who were reacting against regimentation of any kind—they had had it with rules and regulations.

I was given the position of head usher, responsible for seating everyone so that their attendance could be easily checked as present or absent. I was also charged with the responsibility of maintaining the decorum of the services. My brother Hal had been required to serve only 18 months in the army and had then enrolled at Drury one year ahead of me. He became one of my ushers.

I enjoyed the many famous men who came to speak, such as Alexander Kerensky, president of Russia when the communists took over, General William Wainright of Bataan death march fame after Corregidor, and Admiral Hooper of the Pacific naval warfare. One Tuesday, a few minutes after the speaker began, beautiful soft music began to waft out beneath the speaker's voice. I thought, *That's a nice touch. Wonder who thought that up?* A second later the raucous humor of Spike Jones' classic "Tea for Two" burst out! After a moment of shocked silence, the student body burst out laughing and began rocking back and forth, holding their sides, and continued to laugh uproariously as my staff and I ran about frantically looking under pews and peering into every closet, trying to find out where the noise was coming from in order to shut it off.

Finally Hal found the main breaker and switched off all the power in the building! Now all was plunged into semi-darkness and silence—no microphone, no organ, nothing. So the dean of students stood up, apologized to the speaker, and shouted a dismissal to everyone else. Even the professors were chuckling behind their hands as they marched out trying to maintain dignity and decorum. After everyone had left, we found that someone had crawled under the podium, spliced into the wires, and rigged an ancient stereo with powerful old speakers onto a timer, set to go off just as the speaker began. We knew it had to be one of the veterans because only they had the training to rig timers like that, but we never found out who did it.

This incident, coupled with the fraternity joshing, taught me the value of humor. I had been far too serious, desperate to find out what God wanted me to do. I sensed even while we were running around trying to stop "Tea for Two" that just like the professors, God was watching and chuckling, hand over mouth, muffling His glee at the pandemonium.

From then on I sought humor when things became too serious. Years later, in our three-week counseling schools, when the atmosphere became too heavy and tense about the middle of the second week, we would require everyone to attend an extra evening session, at which we would set up a video and play Bill Cosby's "Himself." For two hours the class would roar with sidesplitting humor—and for the rest of the sessions they would enjoy a light and joyous atmosphere. Still today Paula and I play games with our children and grandchildren and take them to comical movies so we can laugh together. One deadly serious prophet came for ministry and then was dumbfounded when immediately after a powerful ministry session I turned on the TV and invited him to play a game of Pac-man. We knew he was being healed when we came home one day and found him sitting on our bed working the remote control, watching TV, and laughing.

## LEARNING HOW TO LET GO—AND LET PEOPLE FALL

Among the Lambda Chi was Hoyt Stocker, who also happened to be one of my five roommates. He was the life of the party and kept us in stitches of laughter. But he absolutely could not wake up in the morning. He and I worked as waiters in the Commons, each having two tables of eight to serve family style. We had to be in the Commons by 7:15 a.m. and have our tables set and ready to go at 7:30. Paul Davis, another ministerial student, was the head waiter and would plead with Hoyt to try to make it on time—to no avail. So he assigned me the task of getting him up and ready.

It was simply impossible! I would pull him bodily out of bed, jostle and shout, everything I could think of, and he would simply fall back to sleep on the floor or wherever I dumped him. I even poured cold water on him. He just shook it off and fell back to sleep. I include this story because it was with Hoyt that I learned how to let go and let people fail, yet not feel guilty that I had somehow failed them. Sometimes, one has to simply let go when people adamantly choose to fail or sin. I doubt I could have survived in the pastorate, much less as a prophet, without a nervous breakdown if the Lord had not written this lesson into me with soporific Hoyt. Hoyt eventually flunked out and left.

Before that happened though, Hoyt and I took a European history class together. The students were seated alphabetically, starting at the back of the room; and so last names beginning with "S" were in the front row while the A's and B's were seated in the back. Rabbi Jacob spoke with a soft mellifluous voice, which was just too hypnotic for Hoyt no matter how interesting. Stocker was right next to Sandford, so I couldn't help but notice that Hoyt kept nodding off beside me. I can remember a specific occasion when he just gave up, put his head down on his desk, and fell into a deep slumber. I saw Rabbi Jacob had been glancing his way as Hoyt proceeded from drowsiness to full-out slumber.

At last I saw that the rabbi was coming to speak to him. I knew that Hoyt's behavior was probably very insulting to the professor and that he had every right to scold Hoyt severely. So I nudged Hoyt hard to wake him up. He looked up bleary-eyed as Rabbi Jacob leaned forward over him and said very softly and kindly, "Pleesse, Mr. Stockie, it iss not already yet time for sleepink. You vait a little while, yess?" The class erupted in laughter. I never forgot Rabbi Jacob's kindness, and from that moment on determined that whenever I was called upon to rebuke, I would try, especially in public, to couch it in the gracious manner of our Lord. That single simple happening wrote more onto my heart than a thousand sermons about kindness could have accomplished.

### LEARNING ABOUT OCHLOCRACY

In the spring of my sophomore year two other events wrote deep lessons into my heart. One night a group of guys from the three fraternities got together and decided to stage a "panty raid." That meant they would find a way into the women's dorms late at night, run in and overturn beds, swipe whatever panties or bras might be hanging out, and just create some hilarious mayhem without hurting anyone or doing any serious vandalism. All of us fraternity guys were rousted out of bed to join in. They figured if a large number of the student body was involved, no one would get into deep personal trouble or be expelled.

Above the Commons had been built a new women's dorm, Belle Hall. A group of us climbed to the roof of the kitchen and entered through a window on the south end. I went along, not wanting to upset beds or steal anything, but tagged along for the fun and excitement— actually thinking I could be there to make sure things didn't get out of hand. I was the head of the ministerial group and one of the "seven sages" (the top seven ranked scholars in each class), so I felt responsible to make sure nothing seriously harmful happened.

The guys raced through the rooms upsetting things and then down the hall to the north. Since none of us had ever been in that new dorm before, we didn't know there was a floor-to-ceiling mirror on the wall just around the corner. So we went dashing around the corner—only to meet a group of guys running right at us! As we turned around, frantically trying to get away, we crashed into the fellows behind us! We could hardly untangle ourselves for laughing after we realized it was actually our own reflections.

From there we went on to gain access to McCullough Cottage, an older larger dorm. We ran helter-skelter through the rooms, teasing and laughing with the girls, and then down the stairs to the front entrance. But instead of exiting through the front door, the lead guys veered into the parlor, threw open a window, and stepped out through the venetian blinds without bothering to open them. As I was near to the last, still acting as watchdog, I stopped and pulled the cord to raise the blinds to prevent further damage. I visited there a while with the dorm mother, Mrs. Giles, apologizing for whatever harm the men may have caused, and then stepped out myself. And there stood Dr. Clippinger, dean of men, pen and pad in hand, exclaiming as each fellow stepped out, "You! I'll see you at 2:30 Tuesday" (or whatever time was available).

But that didn't stop the mayhem; the guys continued on to the remaining women's dorm, Wallace Hall. Some found a ladder and climbed to the third floor and in through a window. The rest of us stood below, watching. We didn't know the dorm had rooms that shared a bathroom between them. The fellows on the ladder saw the dorm mother steaming down the hall towards the room our friend was in, so we shouted a warning. He quickly shoved the bed up against the door to keep her out, but here came Mrs. Haege, a large strong woman, chugging through from the bathroom, mad as a wet hen! Now he had trapped himself. She grabbed him by his jersey, but he peeled out of it and ran back out through the bathroom, leaving her standing there holding his jersey. We all were rolling on the backyard with laughter while we watched him running down past the landings of the stairs with Haege charging after him.

So far, the night had been, for us, just fun. But then, and I have told this story for the lesson behind it, ochlocracy (mob rule) took over, and what had been fun became evil. We wound up marching across the campus, shouting obscenities at the leadership, and throwing handfuls of gravel at the university president's house! Mob rule had taken over and pent-up frustrations had begun to vent, especially among some of the veterans.

No one was expelled, but each of us took a turn meeting a scheduled appointment, getting chewed out. We carried a flag of warning on our dossiers until we graduated—one more misstep and we would be out!

That escapade became an invaluable lesson to me. I learned firsthand how mob rule can take over and rob people of sanity and morals. I knew then how a mob composed of normally upstanding citizens who would never in their rightful mind hurt anyone could become carried away and lynch blacks or do most any kind of harm. I saw how I could go along thinking I was maintaining some order and then be carried away myself, beyond reason or conscience. That created a bit of humility in an otherwise self-righteous ministerial student.

It showed me that reason alone could not deflect the power of ochlocracy. At that time, to me, satan was no more than a figure of unreasoning men's imaginations, but later, after conversion and the infilling, I knew it was satan's power that had made use of our latent, undealt-with resentments to turn innocent fun to destructive vandalism. Never again did I superciliously judge Ku Klux Klan members or other hate groups. Now I had been given a base from which to pity them and grieve for them. This served me well in the pastorate when I would see members in a meeting carried away by whatever the defiling spirit of the moment was, taking them beyond themselves into opposing the Lord they loved. That humbling experience built in me a base of compassion I might never have had were it not for that wild unthinking night.

## A Lesson About Rationality and Philosophy

The second learning experience during my sophomore year did not occur at school. That spring my mother needed to go to St. Louis. She had been diagnosed with a rare eye condition called aneiseikonia. Those afflicted with it see farther with one eye than the other, which somehow creates a light condition between the eyes referred to as "night blindness," and causes terrible headaches. The only doctor who could treat it practiced at Barnes Hospital in St. Louis. Since Dad had to be at work and Mom wouldn't be able to drive because part of the trip would be at night and her eyes would be dilated anyway, we decided that Mom would pick me up in Springfield at school, and I would drive us to the hospital and back.

Our plans worked...until, partway home, I drove up behind a slow moving vehicle in a misting rain. Coming down into a valley, I veered to the side a little to see if I could pass. When I saw a narrow culvert ahead, I attempted to pull back into line. However, as I did so, the rear wheels caught on a patch of mud and spun the car. (Later we learned that in that new Frazer something was wrong with the rear differential so that it gave out and caused the spin.) Going about 50 miles an hour, we turned around backwards, hit the culvert with the right rear fender, and spun over and down to land upside down ten feet below on the creek bank. I saw my mother flying out the door halfway over and turned to catch her—which probably saved my life. I lit on my feet on the inside roof of the car, scrambling out the passenger side door to find my mother.

She lay half under the passenger side of the car. Water was running under and around where I knew her head would be. I was panicked that she would drown before help would arrive. Even though I was a weight lifter at the time, extremely strong for my size, I was not strong enough to lift that heavy Frazer off her. I remember straining at it, frantic and furious that she might drown—and then nothing because I blanked out mentally. The next thing I knew I was carrying her up the bank, and with the last of my strength I lowered her to the soft ground. There was no way I could have rescued her from under that car unless the Lord had given me Samson's strength for the moment! This was the first miracle I had ever encountered, and it began a flame of faith in my hardened philosophical heart.

Another lesson occurred when moments later Mom woke up. "Jack," she said, "Where are we?"

"On the way home from St. Louis, Mom."

"What happened?" she asked.

"We had an accident, Mom; the car rolled over," I replied.

"Was Dad with us? Was he hurt too?"

"No, Mom. He's all right. He's at home," I answered.

"Oh, thank God," she sighed.

A few moments later Mom said, "Jack, where are we?"

I did a double take, and then replied, "On the way home from St. Louis, Mom."

"What happened?" she asked.

"We had an accident, Mom. The car rolled over."

"Was Dad with us? Was he hurt too?"

"No, Mom. He's all right. He's at home."

"Oh, thank God."

A few moments later we went through the same questions and answers again—and at least five or six more times before help and an ambulance arrived.

That event greatly shook my idolization of the conscious mind and the supposed supreme worth of human reasoning. In those days not only liberals but mankind in general were caught up in a love affair with intellectualism and rationality. Human rationality reigned supreme, banishing the superstitions of religiosity along with devils and demons, and science was expected to develop cures for all mankind's warring madness.

This philosophy played itself out differently in the various fields of human endeavor. The watchword in science and economics was "progress." In counseling it was Rodgers's non-directive counseling, which promoted the idea that each man's supposed native goodness and rationality could find truth and freedom. In politics, after the First World War, it created a utopian optimism that we had "fought the war to end all wars." Even the insanity of Nazism, the holocaust, and the horrors of the Second World War had not yet completely smashed mankind's naïveté in its belief that right-thinking rational men could find answers to the world's problems. It took a brutal cold war, the Korean War, and Vietnam to deliver mankind from the delusion of the power of its own mentality, its own rational intellect—to deliver us from ourselves and from all evil.

There in a cold misty rain, miraculously having saved my mother from drowning, and now listening to her mind run in circles, I realized that human reasoning is not enough. There, along that road, I came finally to comprehend throughout my being what one philosopher had said of rationality and philosophy, "Philosophy is a blindfolded blind man frantically searching in a dark room for a black cat that isn't there!"

## MY CONTINUED SEARCH

Okay, so now I knew that rationalism and philosophy couldn't find the answers for me. So maybe mysticism could. I still didn't know that the Lord Jesus Christ is the only Way, nor that it is through the Holy Spirit, prayer, and the Bible that one finds the keys of life. It was then that I plunged more fervently into the mystical things I mentioned before: Rosicrucianism, Edgar Cayce, Gina Cerminara, Madame Blavatsyky, spiritualism, etc. These took me nowhere, but that's where I was going during the summer of 1949.

## MY DEVELOPING RELATIONSHIP WITH PAULA

In the fall when I returned to Drury, I was still going out with Alice, but then some strange things happened. I accidentally overheard Ed Wolfekueler, another ministerial student, talking with some classmates about all the gorgeous freshman girls that had come to Drury that year. Among them he mentioned a beautiful redhead named Paula. When I heard that, my spirit leaped in recognition and joy inside me. I thought, That's strange. What's that?

I soon found out that the Paula he mentioned was another student like me working her way through school by serving as a waitress in the Commons. About two months later, I noticed Paula was dating an "orangutan," a rich guy who I knew by discernment was up to no good, especially in relation to her. One night as I walked across the campus, they crossed in front of me; and as I looked after them, I was dumbfounded to hear my own spirit shouting within me, "Get away from her. That's mine!"

I thought, *That's crazy. Where did that come from?* At the time I was almost engaged to Alice, and everyone thought we were "a number," the expression in those days that meant destined for the altar.

Then another night a few weeks later as I was preparing to leave McCullough Cottage, after escorting Alice to her dorm and making sure she was safely upstairs, I saw Paula through the window beside the door as she was walking in. The orangutan had gotten fresh with her and she was furious. She was walking rapidly with her long beautiful red hair streaming out behind her, eyes flashing with anger, color up. I took one look, and again the Lord spoke clearly and forcefully—so distinctly and powerfully I never ever thought to question it. He had spoken and that was it. "Get free of Alice quick. Paula's free. She's the one."

Now I was in a quandary. There was nothing wrong with Alice. She was a sweet girl and I was fond of her. However, during the summer there had been a restlessness in my spirit in which I had begun to sense that we were not meant to be man and wife. I knew then that I didn't love her in a husband and wife way. But I hadn't known how to tell her. That inner vow I had made never to hurt anyone now did me in. I couldn't tell her God had spoken. No one in our circles believed in that kind of thing in those days. In fact, if you said God had spoken to you, you would have been accused of the highest arrogance and lowest foolishness, "Who do you think you are? To think that the very God of all the universe would take time out to speak to little old you!"

So I couldn't explain to Alice that God had told me to marry Paula. And even if I could have, I thought that might hurt her all the more. So I did nothing—which of course hurt her more than if I had given her any reason at all. I've always felt guilty for just leaving her without saying anything. Years later I wrote her a letter, explained everything, and apologized—but that was far from enough.

I just stopped dating Alice. In the meantime a bunch of Sigma Nu fraternity men began to pick out the tables Paula served and sit there for every meal. They were a rough group who enjoyed giving her a hard time. They would hide bowls of food under the table, claiming she hadn't served them and then send her for unnecessary things. Often they overloaded her tray with dishes until she could hardly carry them. One time as she tried to set a heavy tray down at the counter in the kitchen, she missed the edge and caused a resounding crash as everything smashed onto the floor!

That gave me an entree. By then I was second in command in the Commons and served the faculty tables. They didn't eat as much as the students and usually left quickly, which gave me extra time to help her.

Three fraternities lived on campus: the Sigma Nu, the Kappa Alpha, and the Lambda Chi. We called them the "Sigmanures," the "Crapper Awfuls," and the "Lamby Pies." (By then my finances had become so tight, I had resigned from the Lambda Chi.) The Sigmanures were the athletes of the campus, the Lamby Pies the scholars, and the Crapper Awfuls somewhere in between. Paula's group were the big eaters, the rough-and-tumble tough guys. They loved to bother her, so I became her protector. Actually, they were fond of her and would have massacred anybody who tried to hurt her. After a while they said to Paula, "He's all right. We approve. You're safe with him." I had passed the test.

Finally, after three or four weeks, I asked Paula for a date. We didn't have any money, so we just walked and talked. Or rather, I spouted my philosophical and mystical ramblings for hours, and she listened and said nothing. So I thought she was a wise woman who agreed with me on everything. It was a shock to discover after we were married that she had a mind of her own and intended to use it on me!

I didn't have much wisdom in those days, but I had enough not to tell Paula that God had told me she was "the one." Some men I have counseled have walked up to a woman they were dating for the first time and blurted out, "God told me you're going to be my wife!" Most of those guys never had a chance for a second date! So we just walked and talked.

I would never kiss a girl unless we had dated for a long while. Kisses were sacred to me. After about three weeks or longer Paula finally said, "John, I am a woman, you know!" I responded—and that started the fires. We fought to stay pure, and we learned some more valuable lessons. First, the longer couples date the harder it is to restrain youthful passions. What one can do one week and still stay under control and be able to stop cannot be done safely a week later. Second, once the inner heart says, "This is the one," conscience betrays; it just seems to lie down and quit! Everything inside says it's okay with this one. Only the strength of God's law within us was keeping us out of trouble. We had to learn to date with others, or be with my family on weekends in Joplin, or stay away from extended periods of privacy. It was just too dangerous.

## BANKRUPTCY—AND PAULA'S PAIN

During the spring of my junior year, my parents went bankrupt. Joplin had hit a depression, and the first thing that goes is a gift shop. I announced one morning in the Commons that I might not be able to return in the fall. Paula went to her room and cried inconsolably. That was how she came to know that her heart was completely given and gone.

My parents asked me to quit school and come home to help them close up the shop. I had always tried to obey and serve them the best I could, especially having seen the hurt my brother had caused them. Even while working in the Commons, assisting both the German and English professors, selling clothes after school in a store, and baby-sitting for professors at night—while still managing to make straight A's!—I had been going home on weekends to help clean up the store and get it ready for the next week's business.

But this time I knew in my spirit that their asking was wrong. I said an emphatic "No! I'm called to be the Lord's servant and I'll not turn aside from that calling, even for you." I felt betrayed that Mom, who knew my calling, had asked. Later, when I had studied the Bible more, I knew that my decision was biblically right. But I didn't then, and I just had to stand, hoping that I had chosen rightly.

Paula and I visited in each other's homes a couple times that summer. In the fall both of us continued to scrape by financially at Drury. By then I had proposed and she had accepted, and I revealed to her what God had spoken to me.

## PLANS CHANGE

The Korean War was on. Although clergymen and students for the ministry were exempt from the draft, I didn't feel it right for me to take exemption, so I enlisted in the Navy, to be inducted right after graduation. Paula and I planned to be married in January and finish that school year together. Next I would go into the Navy while Paula finished at Drury. Then I would come back, and we would go on to seminary together.

We knew both our parents were having a tough time financially, so we decided not to burden them with the cost of a fine wedding. Besides, with all our classes and heavy workloads we knew we didn't have the time to plan and prepare for a formal wedding, or even for a simple one. So we did the quickest and simplest thing we knew to do—though we have always felt guilty that we didn't consult with our parents, or at least give them a chance to be there—we just eloped to Arkansas on a Friday and were back in classes on Monday!

We rented an apartment just off campus and I found a job with Heers Department Store after school that paid $20 a week. Ten dollars went for rent and the remaining ten provided just enough to eat on.

Then all our plans blew up! My aunt Tresia sent us a letter that said, "Your brains are too valuable to be wasted on a battlefield, and you are called to the ministry. You go on to seminary." She paid my entire $963 university debt (huge in those days)! So I resigned from the Navy while it was still possible. Meanwhile Paula's plans to finish her degree while I was away in the Navy got blasted by a different circumstance—she became pregnant immediately!

So we finished that year together. I graduated, and we went to St. Louis to live with Paula's parents while I worked to earn money for seminary that fall.

CHAPTER FIVE

# JOHN'S EXPERIENCES WITH SEMINARY, MARRIAGE, AND FATHERHOOD

On September 9, 1951, our first son, Loren, was born. Shortly thereafter I had to leave Paula and the baby with her parents while I went ahead to secure our place at Chicago Theological Seminary. The fieldwork department placed us in South Park Manor Congregational Church at 70th and South Park Avenue in Chicago, within easy driving distance of the seminary at 58th and Woodlawn—but also right in the path of the black migratory wave! The church was dying, as more and more members fled to the suburbs. I was assigned to be the youth pastor and Paula was to be the church secretary.

When Paula and Loren joined me a few days later, we moved into a tiny apartment on the fourth floor of the church, above the gymnasium. We lived in one small room, which served as both living room and bedroom, and had a tiny one-person-at-a-time alcove that held a sink, a small refrigerator, and a two-burner, gas hot plate. Down a few steps was what had been the bathroom facility for visiting sports teams—two dilapidated showers and one toilet. At night, pipes and floor boards creaked and groaned until many times we were sure somebody in that socially deteriorating neighborhood was walking across the gym to come after us!

That first year I made top grades and won the Western Springs scholarship. We resigned from South Park Manor Church, which eventually was sold and became a great church as the black Church of the Good Shepherd. (South Park Avenue, the street on which it was located, was later renamed the Martin Luther King Boulevard.)

The next fall we moved into a makeshift seminary apartment at 5756 Kimbark, two short-end blocks from the seminary. The scholarship paid my tuition with enough left over to pay our rent and buy groceries, so Paula was free to be a full-time mother and I was able to concentrate solely on my studies. (In the next chapter Paula will share more about Park Manor and our new-old apartment.)

### THE PHYSICAL SIGN OF A DEEPER STRUGGLE

When I began studying in my second year at seminary, I found I couldn't read more than a few minutes without brain-splitting migraine headaches. We went to see physicians, optometrists, ophthalmologists, and every other kind of expert we could find, but to no avail. Before the end of the first quarter, I had to resign the scholarship and find a job to support us and pay for the medical bills.

(Meanwhile Paula passed entrance tests, which allowed her to take graduate university courses at the University of Chicago though she had no collegiate degree.)

Now we know that though my eye condition was clearly physical, it was also psychosomatic. I could not continue to read and swallow the modernistic liberal junk that passed for intellectual honesty. My heart and physical system were simply refusing to ingest what I knew to be error and prideful fleshly philosophy of religion rather than faith.

In my first year of study, Dr. J. Coert Rylarsdam had possessed good faith as he taught the year-long course in Old Testament, and Dr. Ross Snyder in the religion and personality department had been an honest and humble seeker after life with God. The course, Early Church History, had also been a blessing. In the second year, however, the professors in New Testament courses worked a miracle every day—they made the most exciting book in the world as dry as dust!

I never could figure out how they could justify much of their convoluted thinking. On the one hand they would teach us that Paul did not write this or that letter, and in the next paragraph propound that Paul believed this or that by quoting from the very letters they had just said he didn't write!

"Form criticism" had become the "in" for scholarship, along with the JEDP Wellhausen theory and "demythologization," each of which attempted to apply scientific formulas for critical examination of the Bible, but were for the most part, as far as I was concerned, merely metaphysical sophistications to justify unbelief. Those professors could simply not believe that men inspired by the Holy Spirit wrote the Bible or that miracles happened as the Bible records, so they set about to find alleged scientific and rational reasons why those things did not happen. They ascribed the miracles of the New Testament to the "superstitious way men thought in those days." I never could understand how they failed to realize that they were calling all the founders of our faith fools and liars, or how they reconciled their reasoning with the fact that those same supposedly benighted flounderers managed to found our Christian faith—which converted millions of people within a few centuries and still grows in glory to this day!

## BREAK US DOWN—BUILD US UP?

At that time, the seminary had developed and announced to all the students its own plan. In the first year they purported to tear down each student's entire faith and belief system. In the second we were supposed to be searching, thinking, and praying, trying to rebuild our faith and theology. By the third year we were to put it all back together so that we could graduate with a mature belief system all our own, disregarding any ideas inherited unthinkingly from our parents or our Sunday school and church. They wanted us to individuate and discover our own belief system.

But many of the students simply cracked! One took a butcher knife and chased his wife, trying to kill her! Another went home to his father's farm a broken and confused man. Several simply packed up and left. Dr. McGiffert, the seminary president, called Paula in to ask, "Is John really having trouble with his eyesight, or is it something else?" Paula was able to tell him honestly that it was just something physical—because that's what we thought it was at the time.

(Even though I feel it important that I speak openly and frankly, I don't mean to criticize harshly or belittle Chicago Theological Seminary. I was carefully trained by my parents and others to honor all authorities, even the erring. So it pains me to speak as I feel I must if my story is to be told with integrity.)

Many of the professors were men of good faith. But liberalism and modernism were well-set into the process of destroying faith in many old-line denominational seminaries, especially obscuring and blocking intimate relationship with God our Father through our Lord and Savior Jesus Christ and the Holy Spirit. These scholars were caught up in forces far beyond the ability of their minds and spirits to handle—strongholds of deception long planned by the forces of darkness.

In the heart-wrenching searching that all this seminary turmoil created in me, I learned some tremendously valuable lessons. Among the foremost was *the clear realization that the mind is the wrong instrument for finding faith*! "God is spirit, and those who worship Him must worship Him in spirit and truth" (Jn. 4:24). My seminary had fallen out of balance. They caught the "truth" part but almost totally missed the "in spirit." I learned on the one hand not to disrespect or disparage intellectualism—most of my peers today regard me as an intellectual—but also never to be caught up in the mind's delusions.

The old-line seminaries knew and said nothing about the Holy Spirit, who is the quintessential and essential conveyor of truth to mankind. Consequently they wandered in oxymoronic labyrinths of intellectualism and rationalism far from who God really is.

Most people in the scholarly world of old-line churches had lost track of the reality of God. We had theologies and theories *about* Him. We had church history *about* Him. However, no one really experienced Him or knew Him. Paul Tillich's concept of "the God above God" was all the rage, as professors and students discussed and debated for hours. Semantically, words *about* God had become confused with God Himself to the extent that *the search for truth had become all there is to God.* The words about God had become God. The search was everything.

One was not supposed to find God. That would be the height of arrogance, to think yourself smarter or more privileged by God than anyone else. Therefore Tillich wanted to find God beyond the idol of thought that men worshiped as God. But in those liberal circles no one was finding the reality of God, and no one was seeing any miracles. *I remember thinking how desperately I wanted to experience something so transcendent and spiritual that my mind could not explain it away. I hungered desperately for reality.*

### UPSIDE DOWN AND BACKWARDS

Finding reality did in fact happen later on, and I was born anew. But when I went among my former classmates to testify of Jesus, they called me a traitor! To them, I had given up the humble quest for truth and had the arrogance and unmitigated gall to say that I had found God! Who did I think I was that I thought the God of the entire universe would take time out to pay attention to little me?! Of all the self-centered arrogance! Never mind that I told them I didn't find God, He found me. That made it all the worse—to think that God loved me personally.

"What about everyone else—doesn't God love them too?" they asked. I responded delightedly, "Yes, that's what the good news is all about." But they could not believe that God acts sovereignly and personally to love specific individuals. To them that would be playing favorites, and of course God would never do that. "Oh, John, you've become self-deluded. You've lost all humility! You're on your way to insanity."

From these experiences I understood the saying that "these men who have turned the world upside down have come here also." The world sees life that way, making crooked the straight paths of God. My classmates literally saw everything upside down and backwards! What was actually humility in surrender to God they saw as pride. What was in fact their own rebellious pride in refusing the Bible and true faith they thought was the "humility of the search."

What was actually factual in the Bible they saw as myth. What was in fact the myth of scientific objectivity they believed was intellectual honesty—they found "factual and rational" answers to their own false questions. What was actually only a confused philosophy of religion they thought was true faith. True faith to them was nothing but delusion and superstition, without "basis in fact," though the true facts of miracles were staring them in the face in the biblical record! (In this I saw what Paula and I later wrote about as the power of corporate mental strongholds, and how to defeat them by prayer.) *Corporate mental strongholds blind, take captive, and control men's thinking.*

I vividly recall sitting down with one of my former classmates after I had been born anew, listening in shock as he said, "You know, John, I've been doing my own thinking. No one has influenced me. I've just thought some things through on my own, and here's what I think: 'I don't believe Jesus was born of a virgin. They just thought that way in those days. I don't believe the miracles happened the way the Bible writes them. It was a superstitious age, before they had the benefits of science and rationality as we have today. I don't think Jesus actually died on the cross and was resurrected. He just fell into a coma and spontaneously revived....' " *That man had not had a free thought in years!* His mind was totally captive. Every thought was entirely predictable the moment the strongholds of modernism, relativism, and philosophy took hold of his mind!

Truly, "where the Spirit of the Lord is, there is liberty" (2 Cor. 3:17b); and where the Spirit of the Lord is not, there is no freedom!

From such encounters *I discovered where and what the warfare truly is—an ongoing battle for the control of men's minds.* You can see this in Second Corinthians 10:5, Colossians 2:8, and Romans 8:5-8.

## EXPERIENCING THE "REAL" WORLD

Because my eyes had given out, that venture into the intellectualism of seminary was gone. The Lord, wanting to raise up His prophet, even before I was born anew, immersed me raw and naive into the secular work-a-day world. I went to work first in the Ford plant in western Chicago, which was not producing cars but was under contract to manufacture jet engines. It was a mammoth building—83 acres under one roof, all one room! And it was as majestically chaotic!

A number of us were hired to track down and organize the tools needed on the line, which was more difficult than one might think. For example, an invoice would record that 18 wrenches had been ordered and received, each numbered by stamped-on numerals. We would find one wrench in stock, and among the great numbers of workers on the line, maybe one or two people would have another wrench—but neither of those wrenches would have the serial numbers of the 18 on the invoice! The wrenches were simply gone—out the door in workers' lunch pails and pockets. That was a mere sample of the chaos that prevailed throughout the plant. Ford had been in production more than six months, and not one engine had yet been produced! This experience went further to destroy my naive liberal belief, which I had been taught all my life, in the supposed goodness and rationality of mankind.

After two weeks I quit that job and went to work for the Studebaker plant a mile or so north of the Ford plant, also under contract to produce jet engines. In contrast, they were well organized and had been producing completed jet engines at a regular rate for several months. I was assigned to a line of six men as their agent, bringing materials and transporting engine parts to them for further assembly, and taking the parts to the next line when completed. And what an education for a young ministerial student! The first person on the line was a handsome young man, married, with two children, and...a cross-dresser! He wore a brassier and panties beneath his clothing. Each night his wife would help him dress as a woman and apply his make-up so he could go out on the streets!

The second man on the line always carried a stack of porn cards and offered to supply all kinds of pornographic smut to anyone who would buy. In those days moral laws were still very strict. What he was doing was both illegal and dangerous; so he would sidle up to people, make remarks calculated to elicit reactions, and test whether it would be safe to offer materials more directly. He seemed to be doing a brisk business.

The third man would crawl inside the boxes jet parts were delivered in and snooze away most of his hours on the job. I remember being astounded when one of the foremen, examining a problem with one of the engines and knowing the sleeper's expertise, said, "I hate to wake Sam up, but would you go get him? He's in that box over there. We need his help with this thing."

I forget now about the other three on the line, but they were just as bizarre.

I realized then that mine had been a sheltered small-town upbringing. Sin had seemed a foreign word, or something one preached about but didn't really think was very prevalent. There were almost no divorces in those days, most people still feared God and held deep reverence for His laws, and in upper middle-class America sin seemed to be something rare that one dealt with in his own heart and nobody talked about. Here, for the first time, I was seeing sin as the norm among people (instead of goodness) wherever men live apart from God. Sin was not rare—it was rampant and was the normal lifestyle of these men. My liberal eyes were being blasted open!

### Learning About Leadership

After a few months, Studebaker switched back to car parts and I was out of a job. I then found work for Delta Airlines at Midway Airport, which was Chicago's only commercial airfield at that time. I worked the three-to-midnight shift as a cargo agent. It was my job to unload and reload all Delta planes, and the other handlers soon began to gravitate to me as their unofficial leader.

Unfortunately, one guy I worked with was overly obnoxious, rebellious, and lazy. All the men despised him. Once, they even locked him up in the belly bin of a Convair airplane being sent across the field for a checkup. When the mechanics heard a knocking, they discovered him inside and let him out. He came back furious, convinced I had done it, though I had only heard about it. He found me beside a plane preparing to send it out, yelled at me, and took a swing at me. I ducked under his swing, grabbed him around the waist, lifted him bodily, slammed him to the pavement, and sat straddle of him. Lifting heavy suitcases had added to my weightlifting strength, and though he weighed more than 250 pounds, handling him was easy. I held both his wrists together in one hand and was ready to smash him in the face when my earlier vow checked me—so I hurt him worse by chucking him under the chin and calling him a baby!

The night superintendent saw what was happening, and since it was absolutely taboo to fight on the ramp where planes and passengers could be affected adversely, the boss sent us both home. I thought surely I would be fired. The next morning the Chicago superintendent of Delta phoned me after having conducted an investigation. All my coworkers had testified on my behalf. The guy who swung at me was fired. On the other hand, Delta had recognized my leadership, and not only did they not fire me, they made me the foreman in charge of the night shift.

Immediately thereafter Delta merged with Chicago and Southern (actually a swallow by Delta). C&S ran south out of Chicago to St. Louis, on to Memphis and on to New Orleans, with several feeder lines in between. The obvious point of merger was the northern terminus, Chicago. We had only two gates, with the distant small C&S gate for emergency operations, and a flood of traffic. Whenever rainstorms swept through—since airports then didn't possess today's sophisticated radar and tracking systems—they had to order many more planes into long holding patterns than they would today. That meant that when weather sufficiently cleared, a great flock of planes would come swooping down into our few gates! We had to work feverishly to turn those planes around and get them into the air again.

Especially during these high-pressure times, our boss acted like a "little Caesar." He never thought of workmen as people. To him they were ciphers. Anticipating what would be arriving after these rainstorms, I would call in for authority to summon additional workers. He would respond, "You got eight units. What's the matter? Can't you do your job?" I never had "men," always "units." So we would be hustling at top speed like ants scurrying here and there while trying to retain safety. I can still hear Mike Dunn, singing out in a fine Irish tenor, "Die for Delta. Die for Delta, dum te dum te dum...."

On the other hand, other bosses at Delta modeled true leadership. I learned more about how Jesus' nature is to be—and is *not* to be—expressed in the work-a-day world among these men than in a thousand sermons or many seminary classes. God was writing into my heart His lessons about life.

### OTHER LESSONS LEARNED AT WORK

The other cargo agents and I developed a great camaraderie, which also taught me a lot about human nature, which in turn became part of the grist mill that ground into me understanding of the Lord and His ways among men. One brute of a man hated all authority and challenged me several times to slug it out with him. I tried tact and graciousness, but to no avail. Finally, I said, "Buddy, I don't want to have to hurt you, but if you force me—I've studied police judo, I've got a family to think of, and I won't mess around with you—I'll just break your back. You think on that." I meant it and could have done it, which he knew from having seen me slam that heavy man to the ground. Apparently, like many bullies, he just wanted someone to stop him. He became my best friend and staunch defender—eventually getting himself fired for punching someone who insulted me.

I learned that turning the other cheek is first a matter of the heart. I had taken his offenses a number of times, turning the other cheek in forgiveness each time, which is never something to be considered namby-pamby. That young man, however, needed me to stop him. Doing so was an act of love, and he knew it.

I learned from another coworker that accidents and humor don't follow logical patterns. Some people just seem to have a knack for getting into funny scrapes and accidents. "Crash" Kutnar was a study in himself.

In those days people paid a dime to mount the stairs and lean against a railing to watch planes come in and take off. One day as a beautiful girl was watching the planes, a strong wind came up, blowing her dress over her head. Kutnar couldn't take his eyes off that sight and drove the company van right into the wing of a DC-3! Thus, he inherited the name "Crash." Anyone else other than Crash would have been fired.

Crash provided lots of entertainment, including a story that happened on a Convair. Convairs were great prop planes operated by two engines so powerful that if one failed the other could easily carry on. They were built with a large baggage compartment in the tail, and a trap door led through the restroom into the galley. Our team would hustle a raised platform up to the compartment, rush the bags out, and go through into the galley before all the passengers deplaned so we could beat the commissary crew to the galley. In those days the airlines used Sealtest round quart ice cream containers for burp cups, so we'd grab some of those out of the seats and fill them with tomato juice, hot chocolate, and coffee, and dash back out. One time Crash stuck the containers of coffee and hot chocolate upside down into his belt, hiding them under his jacket. On the way out he accidentally caught them on the trap door opening, which knocked off the lids. He came jumping and hollering out onto the platform, dancing, screaming, and pulling his shirttail out and his pants down. Our entire crew was rolling on the ground, holding our sides.

There was never a dull moment working with Crash. Part of our task was to unload and load bags, mail, express, and comat (short for "company material"), in that order of priority. Incoming express had to be taken around the end of the field to the express office. During one shift, we had received several Convairs and had much more than we could use of coffee and hot chocolate. So as a gesture of good will, I sent Crash over to the express office with a couple quarts. A few hours later he took another load of express over and came speeding back running for his life. I said, "Crash, what's the matter?"

He replied, "I didn't know someone had vomited in one of those cups I grabbed. When the express guys drank it down and discovered what was in it, they thought I did it on purpose! So when I drove up with the next load all smiles, thinking they'd be grateful, out came this gob of goop smacking me in the face! And then these guys came boiling out-a-there wantin' to kill me!" Crash was still wiping up-chuck off his face, while I and the rest of the crew were attempting, but failing, to keep a straight face.

Those were only a few of the incidents that happened to Crash. In puzzling over why things happen consistently to one and not another, I began to search for reasons, and from that kind of pondering eventually came the discovery of how bitter root judgments and expectancies cause patterns of events in people's lives.

### BACK TO SCHOOL—AND OUT OF A JOB!

Our daughter Ami was born January 23, 1953, while I was still working at Delta. And, as if having two infants, trying to support them, and finding healing for my eyes were not enough, several other things happened that changed my life again. First, Dr. Jessen, a brilliant optometrist who became the inventor of soft contact lenses, found a way to fit me with bifocals that enabled me to read without headaches. Consequently, I enrolled in school again, limiting myself to two courses a semester because more than that was still too much for my eyes.

In the meantime, I continued working at the airport. One stormy night when we were hurrying to turn around several planes, I leaped into a Convair belly bin to hand out the last bags of mail. I didn't know that my helper had left his tug running in neutral. He threw a heavy mailbag, which knocked the shift into gear and sent the tug chugging into the wheel housing of the airplane! Guess which workman did it? Crash Kutnar of course! The accident caused extensive damage and delayed flights while the Convair was being replaced.

The boss, who liked me, was saddened and apologetic as he said, "It's tougher now, John. Not like it was in the old days. We have to hold someone responsible. You were the foreman. There's just been too many little accidents. I've got to let you go." He knew Delta's pressure for speed had made it tough for our guys. He wasn't blaming me, but his hands were tied. I learned then how big business gradually becomes more and more pressured financially and in other ways until humans become sacrificed. This realization helped me to minister to laborers and employers through the years. I knew their language and their concerns inside out. At the time, I considered this action impartially; I wasn't bitter. I was actually ready to quit and find another job that might be easier on me while studying each day and working at night.

## FULL-TIME TAXI DRIVER, PART-TIME STUDENT

So I went from the pan to the fire! I got a job as a Yellow Cab driver on the streets of Chicago on the night shift! Physically, the work was easier, but spiritually, what a baptism! If I thought I had seen a few things at Ford, Studebaker, and Delta, they were nothing compared to what I would see on the streets most every night—most of which I could never talk about from the pulpit!

The week before I was hired, a cab driver had been murdered in a black neighborhood. Now, by law, cabbies had to take people wherever they asked to go. And so if any of the other white drivers— and even many blacks—had to go into the south side black neighborhood, they would lock their doors, roll up their windows, and get out of there without even coming to a full stop at stop signs.

Considering the law of supply and demand, there was plenty of business on that side of town; so I drove in the black neighborhoods as much as chance would allow. My cab driver buddies were aghast. "John, those guys in there will rob you. They'll give you a hard time. And they'll stiff you" (slang for "they won't give you a tip"). But I never was held up, though several drivers from my barn were. One friend had a pistol jammed into the back of his neck, and heard "Gimme your money." Then, "Hey, that's a nice jacket. Gimme that too." Eventually the thief left him standing in his shorts out in the sticks while he drove off with his cab in sub-zero weather. ("In the sticks" was cab lingo, meaning out away from traffic in the suburbs or in the countryside where no one wants to hire a taxi.)

There was an affinity between the black people in those neighborhoods and me. We laughed and joked and swapped stories, and no one ever gave me a hard time. Very few stiffed me, even though they had less money than most white folks. I loved being among them, and they knew it.

This was one of the great conundrums of my life for many years. I puzzled, "Why did I feel safe among black people? Why did they treat me with such deference and respect? Why, to this day, do black people seem beautiful to me, and the rest of us look too pale? Why did I simply like them, and feel at home among them?"

Years later, after Paula and I discovered the power of generational blessings and curses, the questions were answered. I found out that our family had owned slaves, but treated them like family and eventually set them free. They loved each other and the newly freed blacks chose not to leave but instead stayed on to share the farming. My first words were said from behind the skirts of a black mammy, "Dinner's ready." She loved me and gave me affection.

My father had been a Marine in the First World War. His captain had assigned him to guard hardened criminals on shipboard being sent to the front battle lines in France in hopes they would die honorably. However, when the ship docked, the captain called out every name but Dad's. In answer to my father's inquiry the captain only said, "I have no orders for you."

"What do I do?" Dad inquired.

"Just wait here until the war office remembers you and sends some orders." With that, the officer marched the company away and left my teenage dad standing alone on the docks in a war-torn country. Perhaps this also was a part of the Lord's providence, since many of his company were killed and my father arrived at the front only in time for the last battle. If he had been killed, what would have happened to God's plans for me?

As my father looked around on the dock, he saw soldiers from New York unloading ships, dangerous and knife-fighting men conscripted from criminal elements. He stayed away from them. But the black stevedores took my father in, protected him, and gave him shelter and food.

Hebrews 7:9-10 says, "And, so to speak, through Abraham even Levi, who received tithes, paid tithes, for he was still *in the loins of his father* when Melchizedek met him" (emphasis added). This Scripture says that because Levi was in his great-grandfather's loins he participated in Abraham's paying tithes to Melchizedek! Was I in the loins of my father and therefore knew that had it not been for those black men, I might not have had my chance at life?

My father used to love to listen to the black men chant while they worked. Black singing and chanting have always touched me to the core. I know that for some this is too "far out," but I didn't write the Bible—God did. His Word declares that children "in the loins" participate in what their fathers do. Whether others can believe this or not, years later, when Paula and I began using the keys of knowledge that founded inner healing, this realization finally answered the question for me as to why I had such an affinity for black people and felt safe among them. Puzzling and praying about it was part of what helped us discover the keys of generational healing and blessing.

## MEETING A LIVING WITNESS

One experience while driving my taxi among black people touched me more deeply than I could ever describe. Mine was a radio cab and I had received a call late at night to go to a 4800 number on Woodlawn Avenue in the middle of Hyde Park, which was then homes in an island of wealthy white people still living in their mansions surrounded by the black wave. Out from the servants' quarters behind a large house came a frail elderly black woman. When she climbed into the cab I was nearly overwhelmed by the aura of grace and love that exuded from her. It filled my cab, and I felt completely enveloped in the love of God. She told me to go to 51st and Providence, which I knew was at Providence Hospital.

She directed me around to the back, where another taxi stood idling, waiting for us. A beautiful young black woman came running and leaped into our cab to cuddle into her grandmother's arms and cry inconsolably on her shoulder. She had gotten into a fight in a bar and had been slashed under her chin from ear to ear! It was probably a miracle of her grandmother's prayers that her jugular had not been cut and she had not been seriously injured, but she would carry an ugly scar the rest of her days.

I felt her grandmother's love and compassion flowing all about her. It was so powerful I hid the tears that rolled down my face while I tried to appear as though I was not eavesdropping. All the way back to the granddaughter's flat the grandmother just listened and held her while she poured out her story. Finally, there was no scolding or belittling in her voice as her grandmother softly and kindly said, "Honey, didn't I tell you not to hang around with those people?" Her voice held such compassion that even the distraught girl knew she was being asked, "What did you learn, honey? I'm here for you, but is it enough? Have you learned your lesson?" I listened while simple down-to-earth wisdom and counsel and prayers touched the heart of the girl.

The young woman's flat was on the third floor, so I supported the grandmother with my hand under her elbow as she labored up the steps. I can't explain how her dignity and her presence affected me. I felt privileged and honored to be allowed to help. Mind you, by then I had experienced so much that I had become a toughened and hardened cynic. But the grace of God in that little old woman's presence would have melted hardened steel. Refusing the tip she offered, I mumbled a farewell, and went down the stairs a changed man. I *knew* beyond doubting that God is real. I felt His presence for days thereafter. I knew He could reside inside of humble people. *I knew in my heart that there was more wisdom in that little old woman, most likely not educated beyond the first few grades, than in the many-degreed professors I sat under.*

That experience shored me up. I was tired to the bone physically, driving sometimes until two and three in the morning and getting up at eight o'clock for all-day classes. But I was more exhausted spiritually. By then I was steeling myself to read what I hated, memorize what was needful to pass tests, and forcing myself to keep at it for the far-off prize of graduation and ordination. That one hour with that little old grandmother built an anchor in me. It said, "There's a light at the end of the tunnel. There is someone with real faith and someday you'll have it too."

Most importantly, that night ended all the false searching. By then I knew that all those years of reading had reaped nothing but mouthfuls of dust. The second of my two questions, "Who is living the lifestyle of Jesus?" was answered in that little old grandmother. I still didn't know how to find what she exhibited, but I knew the answers weren't "out there somewhere"; they were inside the heart, inside the true walls of faith.

Time and space forbid sharing the hundreds of powerful experiences I had in those two years of driving a taxi at night. Suffice it to say they wrote into my heart understanding of sinful human nature. They showed me irrevocably that left alone mankind does not gravitate to natural human kindness and goodness, as Rousseau and other philosophers and my liberal upbringing had taught me. I saw that without the impact of the Holy Spirit, people swing inevitably to sin and degradation. I saw, unequivocally, how adamic sin permeates and defiles all mankind, until—but for the grace of God—we degenerate into immorality, vice, hatred, and all manner of evil.

By then I had brushed shoulders with so many, at so many levels of society, and found myself liking most and loving all; this realization was not born of bitterness or judgment, but compassion for a race corrupted from the beginning. I suppose the second most cogent effect on me during those years was such an immersion into people that my heart was forever wooed by God's grace to love them. This was not something I could take credit for or be proud of; it was not an active striving on my part or attempting on my own to love. It had just become, by the grace of God, a quietly resident fact of life, something God implanted by immersing me both into sinful humanity and His grace. Like the disciples, who so often did not understand what our Lord said until years later, neither did I comprehend all this at the time. Just as the disciples came to understand many things after His resurrection, so did I, long after the resurrected Lord came to live inside me.

### ONE MORE STORY OF MY OWN SINFUL NATURE

Perhaps one more story—or confession—needs to be shared. Sunday school and church had carefully taught us never to lie. My mother added urgency to that lesson by saying, many times in my hearing, "I'd rather somebody slap me in the face than tell me a lie," and directly to me, "Jackie, an Osage Indian must never let his word fall to the ground." My father would say to me, "Say what you mean. Mean what you say. Do what you say." I set myself to be that way, and was proud of it. The Lord had to shatter that—not the honesty— but the pride.

It became a laughingly repeated coincidence that a young Checker Cab driver and I would arrive at the same place and at the same time so many nights in that huge city. We became great buddies. One late night about 2:30 we found ourselves taken way out in the sticks far up on the north side and met at a deserted cab stand. He would need to "dead head" (drive without a fare) to his near northside barn and I all the way to 51st on the south. Bored and tired, we decided to liven things up by racing each other down Clark Street! So we tore off, pushing to the limit. (All taxis had governors on them that prevented drivers from going faster than 55 miles per hour, but that was still mighty fast for city streets.) After a while he waved and took off for his own barn down another street. I continued on down Clark until I saw the Yellow Cab northside barn. I needed to have something repaired, so I slammed on the brakes, skidded on past the streetcar rails, backed up, and whirled into the barn.

At the check-in window the dispatcher told me their mechanic was busy, so I turned around to leave. There, to my surprise, was a police car pulled up behind my cab, lights blazing! One cop announced, "We've got your buddy, and now we've got you too!"

"Whadaya mean?" I said, "I've been in here for the last half hour, tryin' to get my taxi fixed."

The other policeman patted the hood and said, "Naw, your motor's still hot."

"Yeah, I know. That's why I'm in here. It's been running hot." I turned to the crowd of cabbies who had gathered around and said, "That's right, isn't it? You guys could tell them I've been here quite a while." All the cabbies nodded yes and several piped in with "Sure" and "Yeah, that's right."

Neither policeman was convinced but they knew they couldn't make an arrest stick with all that support. So, one huffed at me, "Listen, buddy, you're a southside cab. You better stay outta the north side or we're gonna getcha. We're gonna be watchin' out for you." And they turned around and left.

I knew the other drivers would support me because they all hated the police who regularly got their breakfasts off us. They'd pull cab drivers over for the slightest infraction, or none at all. The cabbies would palm a couple of dollars and slap the money, hidden from passengers, into the policemen's hands behind their driver's license. Most just took the money, gave the driver a warning to make it look legit, and let the driver go. In those days two dollars bought a great breakfast, and taxi drivers resented being taken advantage of. Only a few policemen handed the bills back with a warning or wrote a ticket.

At the time, I was proud of myself for having thought so quickly on my feet and thwarted the police. Soon after my conversion, the Lord reminded me of that incident, and I had to not only repent of lying but also of my pride, and make restitution by contributing regularly to police survivors and memorial funds. That night, or rather, years later in recollection, the Lord slew my sense of self-righteousness as one who would always tell the truth. I learned that I could lie with the best of them.

## OUT OF SEMINARY APARTMENTS INTO A CHURCH

About that time Paula became pregnant with our son Mark. We were so fertile he was conceived despite what the doctor said was an absolutely fool-proof preventative! But they just didn't count enough fools! Now, we had two children and were expecting a third. Others in those makeshift seminary apartments saw that we were managing both school and kids and were surviving financially, so seminary students started having an epidemic of babies! The dean of students called me in and said, "John, don't you think it's about time you went out and took a church?" He wanted to get that source of contamination out of there!

Paula and I had determined to be missionaries and had applied to the American Board of Commissioners for Foreign Missions. They had assigned us to go to Angola; but because communistic riots broke out in Angola, the Board canceled our appointment, determining not to send any missionaries with young families into such danger zones. So we then said to our Conference ministers, "We'll make it our mission to take broken-down churches and build them up."

Dumb! Boy, did they find some broken-down churches.

In June 1955 we became pastor and wife of the First Congregational Church of Streator, Illinois. It was about a hundred miles out from Chicago on the Santa Fe railroad line. The Conference Minister had warned the people, "This is your last chance. If you give this young pastor a hard time, we'll not send another."

I spent that summer calling on all the congregation members. (In those days every pastor was supposed to make the rounds, calling regularly on his people in their homes). In the fall I began commuting to seminary during the week and serving the church on weekends. During the first year, the railroads gave clergy special half-fare passes, so I traveled back and forth by train, and stayed weekdays in the seminary dorm.

By the next summer, a member allowed me to use a vacant lot for a garden, and a friend taught us how to can products in cans rather than jars, which were more likely to break. We raised and canned a tremendous amount of food. Each Monday I would pack a large box of cans along with my clothes and drive to the seminary. In the basement of the seminary was a small area with a hot plate and a roaster oven, some shelves and a sink, plus a long bar with some high stools, where five of us would meet. Three guys supplemented a little cash to my cans and did the dishes, and the fourth was a professional chef who answered the call of God. His part was to prepare the food, and we all ate together in what we euphemistically dubbed "Ulcer Gulch."

## RESISTANCE—AND FINALLY, GRADUATION!

Taking only two classes at a time was slow but effective. Gradually I was mounting enough credits to graduate. Church history courses were still a blessing and so was Dr. Ross Snyder, but I couldn't help but detest most of the other courses. One that I particularly disliked was a course in theology. I had about halfway completed the research for a theme paper on Schleiermacher when the professor (nameless here for tact) wrote and handed out to the class his own paper—88 theses on his version of theology. I was appalled! It had nothing of faith in it, and was nothing but a philosophy of religion, extremely liberal at that. I'm not proud of what I did, but I dumped my work on Schleiermacher and wrote a rebuttal as my term paper, stating and rebuffing his 88 theses one by one. Actually, his theses were just the last straw for me, and all my frustrations with the modernistic liberal stuff I had been studying came out on the professor.

Though still today I would not retract the content—I know I was right biblically and theologically—what I did was altogether wrong, arrogant, judgmental, and abusive. The professor called me in, so furious that the blood was pounding in his temples. "You haven't learned a thing in my class all semester!" he roared. I don't remember the rest of our discussion. I knew he was right. I hadn't, and didn't want to.

That was the only "D" I received in my entire scholastic career. I wouldn't have blamed him if he had flunked me. Pondering this and repenting for it wrote indelibly into my heart that we can be absolutely right and absolutely wrong at the same time. Many times I have taught prophets that they can have a true word, but if it is not presented in Jesus' loving nature, it is no longer true. It was in that incident that the Lord etched that truth onto the glass of my mirror so I would never forget it.

Finally, in June of 1958, came the glorious day. I graduated from Chicago Theological Seminary!

## CHAPTER SIX

# PAULA'S NARRATIVE ON SCHOOL, MARRIAGE, AND CHILDREN

I n September of 1949 I began my studies at Drury University, Springfield, Missouri. I was attracted to this school because of its high standards and because it was the alma mater of both my mother and my aunt. I, Paula Bowman, had no idea that I would meet my husband-to-be so soon. I had dated a very nice young man for more than two years during my high school days but had ended the relationship because his spiritual orientation and church preference did not in any way blend well with the biblical doctrine I had been taught or with the call I knew was on my life.

John Loren Sandford from Joplin, Missouri, was a junior at Drury, and we met working as waiters in the school's dining hall. I remember watching Jack (the name John used at that time) from across the room and feeling strangely and unidentifiably stirred. I wondered why I felt attracted to the six foot tall, 135-pound intellectual with the crew cut, even though we hadn't even talked to each other. (Later I found that he had experienced the same sort of stirring when he first saw me.)

Meals were served family style at large oblong tables, and each waiter was responsible for two tables. As John mentioned in a previous chapter, the boys from Sigma Nu fraternity consistently sat at my tables. They would tease me by hiding their food and dishes under the table and then pretend that I hadn't brought enough food. I'd go back for more and they'd hide that too. The headwaiter thought he might solve the problem by assigning me to different tables, but no matter where I was assigned, the Sigma Nu guys would be there also. One day they decided to "help" me by stacking my tray with all 16 sets of their dishes, plus empty serving bowls. I managed to carry the tray all the way to the kitchen, and placed it on the counter—almost! I missed by half an inch and it fell with a resounding crash! I had grown up with three brothers who sometimes teased me, so I was not unacquainted with teasing, but this harassment was going too far! I might have to pay for those broken dishes!

From that day on Jack became my "knight in blue jeans" who helped me carry my trays. I was doubly grateful, because his presence also dampened the enthusiasm of the "hide-the-food gang." He was helpful in other ways, too. Sometimes I was a little late setting up my tables for breakfast because I could easily sleep through the ringing of my wind-up alarm clock (even though I had put it inside a metal wastebasket to increase the sound). So Jack started tossing pebbles against the screens of my second-floor window at 6:30 a.m. to wake me—funny how I couldn't hear that raucous alarm but could hear those tiny pebble sounds! And sometimes he would even have his tables set up in time to help me with mine. He did that with a grace that did not negatively challenge the individuation I was going through at that time in my life, and I realized I was truly enjoying his attention and wondered what might come of it.

When I had first entered Drury I visited several churches in the area but was disappointed by the lack of life in each. Then I was invited to attend the weekly meetings of the Student Christian Association on campus where I found some life in the worship, Bible study, and friendships. Jack was a part of that group, and I had opportunity to get to know him. He knew without a doubt that God had called him into the ministry, but didn't really know Jesus at that time. The liberal church he had grown up in had not built for him a biblical foundation, but he was searching sincerely and intensely for truth. Some of that searching had exposed him to what I saw as interesting but very strange philosophies, which led him down blind alleys. However, he didn't seem to get stuck there. It seemed to me that God was faithfully at the end of the alleys, challenging him, turning him around, setting him on a healthier track, and pointing him in a new and godly direction that would eventually lead him to the cross, the truth, the way, and the life.

When Jack and I began to date, neither of us had any money, but we appreciated the beauty of the campus and city park, and the quaintness of what was then a fairly small town. We spent a lot of time walking and talking. John talked and I listened for the most part. Sometimes I would carefully question, or occasionally challenge, but I tried to avoid being argumentative. I trusted that if God had called him and he had recognized the call, God was big enough to straighten him out in the right time and in the right way. So I prayed for him to be what God called him to be and do what God called him to do. But I didn't worry too much about his spiritual life; I was more interested in getting to know him as a person, and I recognized him as having integrity and a good deal more maturity and respect for others than many of the other boys on campus had.

Often our "dates" were at the home of an English professor. We baby-sat his children and also graded papers for him. John still enjoys telling how we would put the children to bed, turn on some music, and study. One evening I fell asleep with my head on his lap, while Puccini's *Madame Butterfly* played "Un Bel Di" (which means "One Fine Day") on the hi-fi set. In those days automatic changers stopped on the last "78" and would replay that record over and over again. So "Un Bel Di" replayed continuously. He says as he gazed at his sleeping beauty's face his heart melted and he knew he was in love. "Un Bel Di" is still our love song to this day.

One of the most enjoyable adventures we experienced together was attending a retreat at a church camp with the Student Christian Association and spelunking. It was a totally new experience for me, and I was not at all comfortable with crawling underground on my knees, worrying about the possible presence of snakes and other creatures resident in Missouri caves. But Jack said he would look out for me. So we crawled along with our flashlights and came to a place where we had to drop off one by one to a deeper level. My hero said, "I'll go first and I'll catch you." He went first, I trusted him, and he caught me, just like he said he would. We came out of the cave covered with mud and jumped into a cold river to wash off, but we did so, laughing. I've been trusting him ever since. We haven't gone spelunking again, but we've certainly jumped into some untested places, come out covered with mud, and then jumped into the Lord's river of life, always trustworthy, coming up together, clean and laughing.

Perhaps the most frightening experience we encountered while at Drury took place on a Saturday afternoon when we, along with several friends, traveled to a place in the country. We came upon a narrow river where a large tree had fallen, spanning the stream, and had become a crossing place for hikers. Deciding to walk on the tree, hanging onto limbs that shot straight up, I followed the first few friends across. As I did so, I stepped on a rotting limb that jutted out to the side and it suddenly snapped! Doing a belly flop I fell 15 feet into the river between two sharp stakes that stuck a couple of feet above the water. It was a miracle that I was not impaled on one or both stakes which were barely far enough apart for my waist to plummet between them.

The others were more frightened than I, because I didn't realize what had happened until I stood up in the water and heard them loudly and anxiously express their concern. John says that half second was the longest and most dreadful time of his life as he watched helplessly while I plummeted towards those sharp stakes! Praise God, I was not injured at all. From that moment on I carried a new level of caution in my heart, and John a new awareness of the providence and protection of God. I do confess that still today caution is sometimes motivated by fear more than by wisdom, and I don't always discern the difference. John is fond of saying, "Relax."

I realized I was in love when in the spring of 1950, John's parents went bankrupt and called their Jack to come home. John had not been receiving any financial support from his parents; in fact he had been sending them some of the money he earned from a half-dozen part-time jobs he was working just to stay in school. He had also been faithfully hitchhiking back and forth from home to school, to help out at their store. I made that trip with him twice, though he insisted I ride the bus. Because his parents were not destitute, nor without ability to work, I was upset for his sake that they would ask him to leave school so close to his graduation; college was prerequisite to seminary, and that to his calling from God.

As for myself—my heart was crushed to think he wouldn't return the following semester. I knew I was in love when I experienced the pain of loneliness his absence would create in my life. As it is, we have now been married for over 52 years, and we have never had a dull moment or a boring day—and are still as much in love as when we began. Both of us miss each other when we are called somewhere to minister singly, and we don't sleep as restfully alone, but thankfully, that doesn't happen very often.

John honestly confesses about the "supremely romantic proposal" he made to me when he was still "Jack": "Everyone is asking me if we're engaged—so I told them we are! Is that okay?" Although his presentation left a lot to be desired, my answer was, "Yes." Fortunately over the years he has learned more considerate and better ways of offering new and important concepts and plans even when he is confident that I will agree with him.

In 1951 our plan was to get married, Jack would graduate, go into the Navy, pay off his college debt while I finished school, then he would come back, and we would go on to seminary together. Several things altered that plan, however: My parents insisted that I finish school *before* marriage, so we eloped. That was not a considerate way of doing things, and was certainly a way of dishonoring our parents in our youthful selfishness. But we did it. We soon asked for their forgiveness and were lovingly and graciously forgiven.

When we notified our parents of our marriage, my dad, although somewhat disappointed, sent a telegram giving his blessing (with his unique brand of humor): "Congratulations. We'll love him even if he is ugly." My parents did show their love to us both in many ways. Even years later, as my dad was developing Alzheimer's disease, he held out his arms to me and said, "I didn't know. I'm so sorry. I didn't have a father—I didn't know." I think he was saying he was sorry that he had been gone so much during my childhood. I hugged him and told him what a wonderful father he had been in so many ways, and how very much I loved him. We hugged each other and cried together.

As newlyweds John and I moved out of our dormitories into a tiny share-the-bathroom-with-your-neighbor apartment across the street from the college library. We set up a simple budget: ten dollars a week for the apartment and the same amount for food, and did laundry by hand in the bathtub. I almost immediately became pregnant, but we finished out the year and John graduated. His aunt, convinced that John belonged in seminary rather than the Navy, gave him the money to pay off his college debt.

We stayed in St. Louis with my folks until our son Loren was born. And the Lord had mercy on our finances there too—only $15 a day for the hospital and $75 for the doctor's fees! My, how times have changed!

I had been enjoying myself at a church picnic when labor began and didn't recognize at first what was happening. I was 19 and healthy, and the doctor had informed me that I could do whatever I would normally do. Feeling quite well, and not expecting the baby for two or three weeks, I decided to play softball during the picnic. It was a strictly for fun game with people of all ages, so I didn't get rambunctious, play hard, or run fast.

After a while though, I began to experience some pains I had not felt before. They weren't the kind that you see acted in the movies, so I went on with the game. Finally I realized there was some regular frequency to the discomfort I was feeling, and so my family and friends whisked me off to the hospital. We discovered I was definitely in labor, and since I was beginning to fear that I had done something that might hurt my baby, I prayed that everything would be okay, and that the baby would be whole and healthy.

After 13 hours of what seemed to be uncomfortable messing around, I was given some kind of a pill that made me sleepy. The next thing I knew I was being taken into the delivery room and given ether. When my mother heard this, she and John were both greatly agitated because our family doctor had informed her when I was a child that I could have a negative reaction if given ether. In those days the medical community had not yet learned that giving gas to a mother could be harmful to the baby as well. No one had asked me any questions about anesthetic or allergies, nor asked my permission.

When baby Loren was brought in to me, after having been kept in an incubator for a while, he was a pasty bluish color and very sleepy. It took quite a long while to wake him up, but he appeared to be unharmed, and I was much relieved. We went home from the hospital to my parents' house. I held our precious baby, nursed him, rocked him, talked and sang to him most of the time. And when I was resting, John or my siblings or my parents lavished lots of affection on him.

Years later, when Loren was in his 30's, he, John, and I were teaching at a seminar in Spokane, Washington. The lesson dealt with experiences that we have while we are still in the womb. I had just finished relaying the story about my foolish softball game when Loren called out, "Stop. I have just been given a revelation! The answer to a question I've always had in my mind!" He went on to say that there had been thoughts and words running through his mind, "If I go to sleep I'll die!" He revealed that as a very little boy he had fought going to bed and to sleep.

John says, "Boy! Did he!" He had to pace with him hour after hour, night after night. Lots of young children fight sleep at one time or another, but Loren's insistence had been abnormal. Even as an adult Loren continued to think of all kinds of things to do to avoid going to bed and to sleep, so much so that it was interfering with his marriage because his wife liked to go to bed early but not alone. He said it had nothing to do with fear of intimacy. It was a feeling he had always felt that if he would go to sleep he would die. "Now I know why that has been plaguing me! It started with the ether! I knew if I fell asleep I would die! And guess what! I have always hated baseball and softball! I thought Mom's playing softball was what forced me to be born early."

(Researchers have now found that babies choose their own time to be born and send a signal to the mother's body that starts them into labor, and that if babies are induced or robbed of their chance to choose their own time, they react in anger!) So, we all prayed concerning his prenatal experience and birth trauma and that he would be healed and set free. Soon after that Loren was able to play with the men of his church in the softball league and enjoy it. Further, he has been able to go to bed at a reasonable time with his wife and to relax and enjoy being there.

## OUR TIME AT SEMINARY

As John wrote in the last chapter, we went to Chicago with a brand new baby so that John could enter seminary.

Park Manor Congregational Church was very welcoming, and I enjoyed my job as secretary/receptionist. Church correspondence, newsletters, weekly bulletins, and the like were in my portfolio. I also typed John's school assignments for him and worked alongside him with the youth. John and I enjoyed singing in the choir. Although I teased him about singing through his nose, he turned out to be a really good baritone.

My office was near the side entrance to the church, and there was a fairly steady stream of people who stopped to visit on their way to meetings. Sometimes they talked with me, but they always took time to admire and talk with Loren who occupied a crib just beyond my desk. A large group of older ladies spent one day a week quilting in a room at the end of the hallway. When Loren began to crawl, he would head for their group as fast as he could go, and they enthusiastically encouraged his coming.

At church gatherings people loved to hold Loren, and he seemed to enjoy being passed around there and at the youth meetings. In order to get more personally acquainted with the youth, we would invite them, one or two at a time, to simple suppers at our apartment. Our little apartment became a safe place for them to pour out their hearts, and the Lord gradually gifted us with His pastor's heart.

## A SECOND CHILD, AMI, WAS ON THE WAY

Shortly before we left Park Manor and moved to Kimbark House, we hosted Dr. Walker Alderton, professor and advisor for fieldwork at Chicago Theological Seminary, for dinner in our tiny church apartment. He was a very kind, wise, and caring person, and a Godsend for us for that evening. While the three of us were pleasantly visiting, I was suddenly hit with excruciating pain. John called our doctor, who ordered me to come to the hospital. So John and Dr. Alderton carried me down two flights of stairs, placed me into our 1939 Ford, and we went straight to the hospital.

Tests showed that I was pregnant, but the doctor was afraid that it could be a tubal pregnancy. I remained at the hospital for ten days with my feet elevated, enduring many tests and the repeated visits of groups of interns who were all wondering if surgery might be in order. John and I were stressed both about my physical condition and how we were going to pay the hospital bill without insurance. We prayed as well as we knew how.

Finally the pain disappeared and I was released from the hospital. I carried our daughter Ami full term without complication. Thank God that hospitals charged very little in those days—so little that couples often placed their elderly parents in hospitals for a few days while they went on vacation.

## Into Seminary Apartments

Our seminary apartment in Kimbark House consisted of two and a half rooms on the second floor of a mansion that had been divided into small apartments to accommodate married seminary students. We shared a bathroom, refrigerator, and vacuum cleaner with the apartment next door. Everyone in the house cooked on hot plates and in small roaster ovens, and we had to let our neighbors know when we were consuming electricity lest we blow fuses. In order to use an old-fashioned wringer washer, everyone in the house also had to sign up for laundry time. We hung our drying laundry on lines in the basement. The whole operation was an exercise in consideration. Our bed was one that we let down out of the living room wall. Ignoring the many varied sounds coming from next door was also another exercise in consideration.

When I started into labor with Ami, John was working for Delta Airlines and could not possibly get home in time, so our downstairs neighbor, Charlie, drove me across town to the hospital. John made it to the hospital just as I was being admitted. However, the admitting desk attendant, being completely occupied, was not giving me immediate attention. I finally called to her in a loud voice, "Do you want me to have this baby right here in the lobby, or would you rather I go upstairs?"

Immediately she called for a wheelchair, and Ami was born in less than 15 minutes with no time for prep. Our second child was delivered by a Polish woman doctor who was completing an internship in order to be fully licensed in the United States. John barely had time to sit down with a magazine before the nurse came to announce, "You have a girl." My doctor arrived soon after. I went home in a couple days to find Loren sitting in his highchair in a neighbor's apartment with his plate of food turned upside down on top of his head. A few days later my doctor was kind enough to come to our home to make sure all was going well.

John was a loving husband and father, but studying and attending classes all day and working a night shift made it difficult. I especially worried about him when he was driving a cab in dangerous places.

Loren and Ami were only 17 months apart, and my life was very busy. In addition, Loren had the yearning to explore, and by the time he was two he managed twice to get through the front door. He always wanted to see the "birdies." Once we found him beginning to climb the fire escape on the student apartments across the street. Another time we were searching frantically everywhere for him when a call came from the chaplain of the University Chapel (where John was serving as a chaplain to the youth group). The chaplain had recognized our little boy when the police picked him up nearby and delivered him to the chapel, and he immediately called us.

"I have a little boy here who belongs to you," he said. Loren had been running happily in the grass in the middle median of the Midway Plaissance! We might have lost him, and we knew it was a miracle of God's providence that he was returned to us so quickly and unharmed. This was another plank God built into our bridge of faith.

We decided to spend some time trying to discover how Loren had escaped the apartment building. We had allowed Loren to play in the upstairs hallway with a little girl in the next apartment, and we just couldn't understand how Loren could have opened the outside door, which was wooden and extremely heavy. Later a neighbor downstairs admitted that he had opened the door for Loren, and we asked, "Why?"

Our neighbor, one of those scholastic geniuses who hadn't an ounce of common sense, replied, "He wanted to go out, and he looked like he knew where he was going." Loren at age two possessed the vocabulary of a four-year old, and seminarians had fun testing his ability to repeat words such as "existentialism," but this was scary!

Loren insisted that he could go to the bathroom by himself, and twice we had to call the fire department to rescue him from the bathroom because he had locked himself in. Ami followed in his inquisitive footsteps as soon as she could walk and got her foot stuck in a basement drain while I was hanging our laundry. For a while we thought we might have to do something desperate, but I finally persuaded her to point her toes while I lifted her leg. Other than that, we had fun with games, stories, and rides to the park in a little red wagon on sunshiny days. Loren soon decided he was the one to pull the wagon, but we had to watch him carefully lest he spy some birdies.

When John had to drop out of seminary until his eyes could be properly fitted with lenses and his headaches stopped, I was delighted to have the opportunity to go back to school, especially since the tests I took allowed me to take graduate level courses at the University of Chicago. My parents were able at this point to help with tuition. I completed a full load of courses and did homework at night after the children were asleep. Somehow, between the two of us,

John and I managed our schedules so that the need for baby-sitters was eliminated.

I did appreciate it when the wife of seminary president McGiffert came from their house next door to graciously offer any help I might need—cooking, laundry, cleaning, baby-sitting, or whatever else. She was worried about my taking on such a heavy load, and she knew that many students crash emotionally. I sincerely thanked her, but never felt the need to call her. I do remember once accepting an offer from Dr. Ross Snyder and his wife to care for our little ones so we could enjoy a special night out.

I spent a summer working in the central administration department of the University of Chicago as a research associate—reading numerous daily newspapers, spotting references to activities and honors of the school's supporters, and recording those items in the files. When the fall term began, I was allowed to take much of the typing home with me. I also painted 25 to 50 posters at a time for various university groups to advertise their activities in store windows and on a huge "mail tree" in the area. Again and again our trust in the Lord to provide was increased—we saw how my continually drawing on everything as a child was preparation for our life and ministry.

During the summer, two of my brothers came to stay with us and found employment. Life was not all labor though. We all enjoyed time off on the nearby Lake Michigan beaches, and in the nearby museums. Several times John and my brother Jerry did frighten me when they swam out into Lake Michigan so far I could hardly see them. At those times I reminded John he was the only husband and father of our family. They finally took my warnings seriously and consented to swim only along the shore—all the way from 57th Street to 81st!

## Out of Apartments Into a Church

When I became pregnant with Mark, the dean called John in for a conference. It seemed that since we had children and were managing home, work, and school fairly well, other couples were following our example. In fact, a couple downstairs were expecting triplets! Unfortunately, Kimbark House apartments were not designed to house so many. To stop the population explosion, the dean suggested that John accept a pastorate and commute to school. We honored his request and began to minister at Congregational Church (which became United Church of Christ) one hundred miles away in Streator, Illinois. It was a rather long commute, but it worked. John drove to Chicago for the week and was home on the weekends. We were paid only three thousand dollars a year, but that was more than we had lived on previously.

One church member allowed us some land to plant a garden; another gave us cherries from her trees, and we enjoyed a cherry-pitting party. We canned all our fruits and vegetables, and John carried boxfuls with him as his donation to the meals that a group of seminarians shared in a little basement room they called "Ulcer Gulch." He loved what time he had to garden and ignored the criticism of a few who thought it was undignified for a pastor to be walking home from the garden in his bare feet.

The children and I were lonesome for him during the week, though we were busy. It was especially difficult for Ami because there were no little girls on the block for her to play with, and Loren, the love of her life, was too often busy playing with his little boy friends who didn't want a girl to tag along.

I was pregnant and without a car, so the children and I made good use of our red wagon as we walked a couple blocks and back when we needed something from the grocery store. It was about an eight-block walk to and from the church, so between choir practice and weekday church meetings, I got plenty of exercise. I also prepared the church bulletins and kept track of phone calls. John was home to preach, make home and hospital calls, and meet in our home with the youth. (We still hear from some of those young people.)

The parsonage was a small but attractive brick house. However, it was totally lacking insulation and was very difficult to heat with an antiquated coal furnace. We were fortunate just to get the temperature up to 55 degrees in the winter. One day we decided to be as the Bible says, "Shrewd as serpents, and innocent as doves" (Mt. 10:16b), by inviting the church's board of trustees to hold their meeting in our home. Very soon thereafter insulation was installed, at least in the attic, and a modern automatic stoker was added to the furnace.

Loren added humor—and embarrassment—to us on one particular occasion when we, being delighted with our family and our nice little house, decided to invite the deacons to meet in our living room. In the middle of the meeting, Loren sleepwalked right through them into the kitchen, and in full view of the deacons, opened the basement door and peed down the steps! So much for pride!

### Learning to Listen to the Lord and
### Follow His Directions Whatever the Cost

In the next chapter John will talk about graduation, ordination, and how we received the baptism of the Holy Spirit. Akin to these experiences was a way in which we had gradually learned to listen to the Lord. We had been reading the Bible more and more when Philippians 4:6-9 leaped off the pages at us:

> *Be anxious for nothing, but in everything by prayer and supplication with thanksgiving let your requests be made known to God. And the peace of God, which surpasses all comprehension, shall guard your hearts and your minds in Christ Jesus....whatever is true, whatever is honorable, whatever is right, whatever is pure, whatever is lovely, whatever is of good repute, if there is any excellence and if anything worthy of praise, let your mind dwell on these things. The things you have learned and received and heard and seen in me, practice these things; and the God of peace shall be with you.*

We began to recognize our need to spend more time in quietness, practicing feeling the presence of God and learning to hear His voice more accurately. We knew that He speaks through His written Word to everyone with eyes to see and ears to hear, but we hungered for specific focus and appropriate applications. We decided to believe that God is able to look into His thousands of biblical gems and call our attention to whatever He wants to make us aware of at a particular time. Together we prayed and listened for chapter and verse numbers, not knowing beforehand what they said. The first time we tried this I was amazed and delighted to receive the Lord's direction to read Philippians 4:10: "But I rejoiced in the Lord greatly, that now at last you have revived your concern for me; indeed you were concerned before, but you lacked opportunity."

From that time till this present day, John and I have held our daily devotions by first worshiping the Lord, then asking Him to cause us to think of Scripture chapters and verses, knowing that He can write on our minds and hearts what He wants us to see for that day, so that we might pray and be ready to act according to His purposes. We share these Scriptures aloud, and discuss and pray about what they might mean. Is He calling for repentance, forgiveness, blessing, protection, healing, comfort, conviction, warning, change...or what? And then we listen a while for any direct words from the Holy Spirit. Perhaps He has good news He wants to share. Or sometimes He may be calling us to minister to Him by sharing His sorrow (see Phil. 3:10). Whatever He talks about, we pray accordingly, and record it in our prayer notebooks for later reference. Sometimes the Lord lets us know specifically who we are called to pray for, and sometimes it may be a general call. Often we have prayed a general prayer and have found later that someone was clearly ministered to as a result. Sometimes we have had a sense of whose burden we are asked to carry, and soon it was confirmed.

In each church we have pastored, there has been a core group of people who have felt called to be intercessors and have truly wanted to learn to listen to the Lord. We have often invited them to join us in morning devotions. When a group of people listen and find themselves receiving similar messages, or fitting together parts of a central theme, accuracy of listening is beautifully confirmed, and the power of prayer is enhanced.

Sometimes miracles of healing have originated in the Lord's prompting and guiding such prayers through groups. For example, our group was directed to pray for a little boy who had been diagnosed with a severe case of pneumonia. Because X rays had shown his lungs to be full of congestion, local doctors felt ill-equipped to treat him, thereby directing his parents to take him to specialists in Chicago. John drove the parents and the boy to Chicago, and the prayer group prayed constantly. When the boy arrived, the specialists couldn't find a trace of the pneumonia and sent him home!

This was a time of great rejoicing for the people of faith in the congregation. On the other hand, we were trying to convert an erstwhile liberal church, and for some in the church that miracle was only threatening. They were terribly afraid of such a real and powerful God and were not ready to fully commit themselves to such an awesome Lord. At one time, one couple called and asked John to come to their home to answer questions. After a while the wife said, "Reverend Sandford, what you are saying is that it's real, aren't you?"

John responded, "Yes. Jesus and our Christian faith are very real." That family never came to church again! They didn't want God to be that real. The church was supposed to marry them, bury them, and make them feel good. But a God who is real has to be responded to and obeyed. So they left. On the contrary, the boy's family (the one healed of pneumonia) was full of gratitude, and eventually his father became a fine Methodist pastor.

We wanted to see the whole church set on fire for God and received a good deal of criticism for our efforts from part of the congregation who didn't want to hear about the Holy Spirit, being born anew, healing, or altar calls. "Do you mean to say I'm not a Christian?!" As Jude 1:10 says, "These men revile the things which they do not understand." We experienced the painful truth of that, but we soon realized that our responsibility was to learn to recognize the readiness of some of the people to see, hear, and understand; to minister to them whatever was needed for individual and corporate growth; and to continue to minister to them despite what unbelievers might say. We didn't want our concern for the scoffers to become critical judgments that could possibly set the hungry ones back.

Ecclesiastes 3:1 is clear: "There is an appointed time for everything. And there is a time for every event under heaven." We pastored that church for six years, until His appointed time came for us to leave. During that time in Streator our sons Mark and Johnny were born. Before we moved on, John prophesied, not in bitterness but in compassion and grief, that if the church did not repent for its having reviled the work of the Holy Spirit, and earnestly seek the Lord, they would someday no longer be a church; instead a filling station would occupy the corner where the church sat.

The Holy Spirit told us before we left that we would be vindicated, and we were—20 years later! We were invited by a Lutheran pastor and a Catholic priest to teach at an ecumenical meeting in one of the Catholic churches in that town! The inter-church cooperation in itself indicated God had been at work to change the hearts of the townspeople, and to enlarge the hearts of those who had stood with us. Many of our former church members attended, even those who had given us a hard time, and we were greeted with warm welcoming hugs and tears.

What did we learn? When God makes a promise, He will keep it—but only in His time and in His way! When we inquired about the state of our former church, we were told that it had continued for about six years after we moved away, and that it had not become the filling station described in John's prophecy; instead, it had become a restaurant. The beautiful stained-glass windows we had admired and loved were now in the local Presbyterian church, and our congregation had been scattered in many directions.

Painful as that experience was to us, it still blesses us to hear from time to time from some who were a part of the prayer group and/or the youth group who are still praying and living for the Lord. Several years ago a couple from that church who had moved to Arizona came to see us in North Idaho, asking John to preside as they repeated their marriage vows on their 25th wedding anniversary. It was a joy to see how they had continued through all those years to grow in their relationship with the Lord.

Learning to listen, trying to evangelize sophisticated modernistic liberals, and suffering persecution and rejection taught us more than any books or classes could have. It wrote onto our hearts how much Jesus endured for us, and it taught us about His patience in continuing to love and accept such rebellious children as we all are.

CHAPTER SEVEN

# WHEN THE HOLY SPIRIT FELL
# AND PROPHETIC MINISTRY BEGAN

(JOHN CONTINUES THE STORY)

In July 1958, I was ordained by the Fox River Association of the Illinois Conference of Congregational Christian Churches. At last, I had done what I had to do to earn my degree and was ordained.

After that I made a decision. It didn't matter that seminary had taught me one couldn't believe the Bible; I resolved that I would believe it cover to cover! I set myself determinedly to believe once and for all that Jesus was indeed born of a virgin; He is the very Son of God our Savior; the miracles did happen as the Bible records; Jesus was resurrected from the dead; and we do have to be born anew.

There were no spiritual fireworks at the time. I just decided that even if believing all that was a delusion, it was the happiest one going, and I would risk everything to believe these things and never turn back. At first, my thinking was a purely mental leap of faith, which went against all my upbringing in the liberal church and my scholarly training in a modernistic, liberal seminary.

Later, when I came to understand the necessity and power of intercessory prayer, I realized that Paula's parents and many others must have been praying for me for many years, or most likely I would not have made such a radical turn to faith.

In the fall of that same year, the Holy Spirit fell on me in my sleep—He had to bypass the interference of my analytical mind! I woke up speaking in tongues and didn't know what it was. In the morning I went to see my friend, Reverend Wilbur Fogg, the Episcopal rector, and told him what had happened. He laid back his head, roared with laughter, and said, "Hallelujah! We've been praying for you for two years!" Wilbur immediately asked Paula and me to join a small ecumenical prayer group, and Paula also quickly received. There were Episcopalians, Methodists, Presbyterians, and a few others, whose churches were as dry as mine, finding fellowship and feeding as they studied the Word and prayed together.

Two weeks later I began to feel fear—of *what* I didn't know. I went to see Wilbur and found him in the sanctuary of his church. He turned and playfully cast a sprinkle of holy water at me. Never in my life had I seen anything so terrifying! It was as though globules of fire were cascading onto me. That began a mighty deliverance session. Those researches into mysticism and the occult had exposed me to the demonic and I had become demonized. However, I had possessed enough moral strength that the demon had enjoyed little access to express; it was as though it had been encased like a tuberculin cyst. But when the Holy Spirit came in, the war was on. The Holy Spirit would not allow that unclean thing to remain attached to me so near His domicile.

Wilbur and his wife Alice came to my house that night. Anticipating a struggle, we had sent the children off to visit overnight with friends. Alice was more gifted as an exorcist than Wilbur and began to call that spirit to surface and be gone. I roared like a lion, and the entire house got "busy." All four of us felt spiritual forces warring all around us. Our cat went berserk, running here and there about the house. Three times it jumped onto the piano and hit the same note on the keys resoundingly. The thought went through my head, from my studies in Shakespeare at the university, "Hear it not, Duncan, it knells for thee" (when Macbeth was plotting Duncan's death and a bell rang out).

At last Alice said, "All right, you've had your little demonstration. Now just calm down, and come out of John, in Jesus' name." It left, and I renounced all magic, witchcraft, occultism, demons, and satan—and was free.

At that time, and still today in many places, much debate circles around the question of whether Christians can have a demon. I firmly believe no Christian can be possessed. Possession occurs when the demonic has totally submerged the original personality and only demons are in control of the person. The Holy Spirit inside of Christians will not allow that to happen, unless an individual persistently renounces the Lord and his faith, and opens himself fully to the demonic. But I know firsthand that Christians can be demonized and even, to limited degrees, inhabited—because I was. I have cast demons away from Christians literally thousands of times in more than 40 years of ministering since that night.

Shortly after that night I called on a lady in my congregation. I knew something was wrong when as I entered her house she said, "This time you're not going to be beheaded, John!" I did a double take and began to ask her questions. It turned out she held hidden animosity towards her son, and rather than admit to those feelings, she made herself believe her son was Jesus. She was therefore mother Mary, and of course that meant I was John the Baptist.

At that moment I was still recoiling from the shock of my own experience with the demonic. All my life I had been told that satan and his hosts were only figments of superstitious mentality, mere projections of evil by ignorant men. Shards of that broken and false pot about the demonic were still ricocheting throughout my erstwhile liberal mentality. So I was loathe (because of fear) to admit that here might be another case. I stammered a few words of hopefully polite conversation and ran to get Wilbur, who soon brought Alice. Alice immediately went after the demon by asking questions, "Did Jesus come in the flesh?"

That tiny woman's head swiveled and out of her came a deep powerful male voice, "*Naw!*"

"Did He die on the cross?"

"*No!*" came the same booming voice.

"Was He resurrected from the dead?"

"*No!*"

With Alice leading, the three of us cast away the demon and prayed for the woman's comfort and healing.

Truth had now leaped off the pages of the Bible at me. Gone were any thoughts that I might have been entertaining delusions when I decided to believe the Bible. I *knew* then that what the Bible said about demons and satan was not poetic or figurative or even, as my teachers had said, "the superstitious way men thought in those days." All of it was factually true, just the way the Bible said it!

Everything was new to us. This was at the very beginning of the coming of the Holy Spirit on the old-line churches. There were no books. There were no cassette tapes or videos. (They didn't even yet exist.) No teachers from old-line churches had yet arisen. To my knowledge, Dennis Bennett, who also had attended Chicago Theological Seminary just ahead of my time and who had then become an Episcopal rector, my friends Wilbur and Alice, a very few others, and Paula and I were the only old-line ministers who had received the Holy Spirit. Here and there a few lay people also had the baptism of the Holy Spirit.

When the Holy Spirit began to fall on the old-line churches, they were in sorry shape—scattered and dead like the dry bones of Ezekiel 37. They were still struggling to get free from rationalism—everything had to be explained rationally if one were to believe it. The watchword was, "If you can explain that to me rationally, then I'll believe it." That was wrong, and backwards. It was Gnostic. A Christian believes by grace, and maybe God will explain rationally—and maybe not at all. No one could ever explain the Trinity, for example. Some things remain mysteries, and we just have to simply believe.

Old-line Christians in those days read their horoscopes in the morning paper and thought nothing of it. Or they went to see "Aunt Fanny" to have their palms read or attended a seance just for the fun of it, blissfully ignorant of the dangers and sins involved. The entire old-line church was not yet biblically grounded, as its charismatics would become later on.

I determined to know nothing except Jesus Christ, and Him crucified. I immersed myself in the Bible for three years, grounding every thought and emotion in His Word. Whatever wasn't scriptural

I threw out, ruthlessly. In prayer I said, "I don't want my mind. I don't want what I've learned in seminary or anywhere else. I want only the mind of Christ. I want all of my mind to be filled and governed by Your Word, Lord Jesus Christ." That has proved to be one of the most blessed disciplines of my life.

My friend Wilbur was still reading and searching for more truth anywhere and everywhere. I remember visiting him, taking hold of him by the shoulders and pleading with him, "Wilbur, will you please stop reading all that stuff? Please determine to read nothing but the Bible for a while." The devil was counterattacking the move of the Holy Spirit on the old-line churches and I knew it. Wilbur didn't listen to me and after a while fell out of ministry altogether.

Proverbs 13:20 says, "He who walks with wise men will be wise, but the companion of fools will suffer harm." I made it a high priority to spend time with other pastors who were richly informed and grounded in the Bible. One such man was Pastor Ed Bender of the Open Bible Church. Hobnobbing with him and some of the evangelical pastors was deeply rewarding and taught me to ground everything of the prophetic and of inner healing in the Bible and sound theology.

Allow me to digress here for a moment to share a humorous story. One Sunday night after Pastor Bender's services were concluded, I went to see Ed for wisdom about some questions. The church was dark, so I knocked on the parsonage door. His wife said, "Ed and his head deacon are over there praying at the altar in the dark. You can still get in through that side door down by the altar."

Not wanting to disturb their prayers, I slipped in, closed the door quietly, and slowly tiptoed toward them in the dark. I didn't realize there was a translucent pane in the door behind me and a street light just outside the door casting a glow of light all about my head and shoulders. When I came within a few feet of the deacon, he heard me and looked up. His eyes shot wide open with fear, and in a shaky voice he shouted, "Oh, my God, it's Jesus!" Tempted to play with that for a while, I stood there silently, enjoying the shock, and finally said, "No, son, just His servant."

## MEETING AGNES SANFORD

In 1959, before Wilbur lost his faith, Agnes Sanford wrote to him saying she was scheduled to speak at Evangel College in Springfield, Missouri, which was then the mecca of narrow fundamentalism. She intended to bring biblical revelations that would crack open long-closed doors and wanted him and Alice to come as intercessors. They invited me to go along.

I had read several of her books, but that was the first time I met Agnes in person. She taught from Genesis chapter one so powerfully that we could almost physically see scales falling off the students' minds. Afterwards we asked her to pray for me for my continual back troubles. She knelt, placed her hands on my lower back, and prayed for me to be enabled to forgive my mother. Waves of power flowed from her hands throughout my back.

Having read about her beliefs, I knew she thought that psychosomatically my resentments toward my mother were a major cause of my back problems. From that night onward, as I discovered more and more things to forgive, my back was gradually healed. That was my introductory experience of inner healing, and it began the searching and experiences that became foundational for many in the area of inner healing.

Agnes and I began to correspond. In 1961 she invited me to be the chaplain at a School of Pastoral Care to be held in Canton, Ohio. I did so. Later Agnes decided to offer the first Advanced School of Pastoral Care. Only those who had previously attended a School would be allowed to come. Because I had been the chaplain in Canton, she invited me to be chaplain in the Advanced School, to be held in Whitinsville, Massachusetts.

By then Paula and I had moved and had become the pastor and wife of the First Congregational Church of Council Grove, Kansas. Reverend Paul Cecerly of the United Pentecostal Church had become my friend (though we often debated about his theology). He was also a tree surgeon. So I worked with him, cutting and trimming trees, in order to earn the money for airfare, room and board, and tuition for the school.

Shortly before flight time, the third teacher at the School had to cancel out. Consequently, Agnes phoned and asked me to replace him. So it happened that my first teaching outside the local church was to mature, highly knowledgeable pastors and church leaders in the first *Advanced* School of Pastoral Care!

### LEARNING BALANCE AND DISCERNMENT

At the second Advanced School held a year later, the Lord used His humorous coincidences to humble and teach me again. We were workaholics in those days; we taught two sessions each morning, counseled people all afternoon, taught another session in the evening, and then counseled again until midnight! And we kept up that schedule the entire week!

By Thursday, I was exhausted—and too full of zeal and lacking in experience to know what fatigue can do to common sense and good judgment. I became carried away with eschatological speculations about the endtime. In fact, I knew the world was going to come to an end that very afternoon at four o'clock, and only those of us at the seminar were going up! I came down to a prayer meeting and sat there sobbing, answering only that something terrible was about to happen. One wise man said, "You know, John, I think the best thing we could do right now would be to go out and get an ice cream cone."

That was probably good common sense. But I thought, *Oh, you poor fool. The world's going to end in two hours, and all you can think of is an ice cream cone!*

Seeing how distraught I was, they sent for Agnes. She took one look at me and said, "John, you're too tired. Go up to bed."

I thought, *The world's coming to an end, and that's all you can think of to do?!* But then I thought, *I can take off from there as well as any place else, so why not?*

What I didn't know was that Whitinsville, Massachusetts, had a volunteer fire department that was called into action by a great bullhorn. Wouldn't you know, right at four o'clock there was a fire, and that great horn sounded out a mighty blast! I shot up off the bed, exclaiming, "Oh my God, it's Gabriel!"—and of course fell back and thought, Oh no, He's come and gone without me! But then those cool bed sheets felt so-o-o good, and I fell asleep laughing at myself.

That experience proved to be invaluable. It taught me much about keeping balance and about discernment. From then on I knew how to tell when delusory thoughts were slipping in—by the unrest and sweaty Mentholatum feelings that came with them. The peace of the Lord that settled in afterwards told me much that contrasted delusion and the Lord.

I learned what fatigue could do to judgment. And since I had to teach that evening, I also learned how open confession enables understanding and acceptance. I had not lost the people's respect, but gained it by demonstrating how I handled embarrassment through faith in the Lord Jesus Christ. And I saw firsthand how the Lord turns our dirty water to best wine for the feast.

I taught with Agnes Sanford for many years, until 1969; then the Lord took us in different directions.

## Leaving the Pastorate

On January 1, 1965, Paula and I began to pastor the First Congregational Church of Wallace, Idaho. During the nine years we were there, I traveled six times a year to speak, and pioneered teachings both in the prophetic and in inner healing. Many people began to fly in from all over the USA and Canada for a few hours of counseling; and miraculous deliverances and healings, both physical and inner, happened frequently. However, those many requests were eating up my time and energies, and I began to feel as though I was giving the children's bread to outsiders. My church was paying for a full-time pastor and receiving only part-time service. I cried out to God, "Lord, You've got to take a hat off me. I can't be prophet, counselor, healer, intercessor, and pastor all at once."

In July of 1973 He responded by ordering us out of the pastorate. He said, "You are to move to Coeur D'Alene, Idaho. You are to write, teach, and counsel, in that order. You are to write seven books for Me." He gave us the titles: (1) *The Elijah Task*, (2) *Restoring the Christian Family*, (3) *The Transformation of the Inner Man*, (4) *Healing the Wounded Spirit*, (5) *The Renewal of the Mind*, (6) *Healing the Nations*, and (7) *The Healing of the Earth*. Six have now been published, plus seven others, and I am writing the originally ordered seventh now.

In 1974 we founded Elijah House, a ministry mandated by Malachi 4:5-6 and Matthew 17:10-11.

With the help of a fine lawyer in the Wallace church, we had applied for 501c3 nonprofit organization papers and received them in April 1975. Our "validation" has never been anything other than the fruit of the Holy Spirit and the truth of His Word (though my degree is a Master of Divinity in Christian counseling). But the 501c3 gave us standing in the government's eyes, to operate as a ministry and receive financial gifts. "Elijah House" (School of the Prophets) was the ministry name the Lord gave us, along with two Scriptures that described the call.

The first was Malachi 4:5-6: "Behold, I am going to send you Elijah the prophet before the coming of the great and terrible day of the Lord. And he will restore the hearts of the fathers to their children, and the hearts of the children to their fathers, lest I come and smite the land with a curse."

The second was Matthew 17:10-11: "And His disciples asked Him, saying, 'Why then do the scribes say that Elijah must come first?' And He answered and said, 'Elijah is coming and will restore all things.' "

We understood from the beginning that we were called to minister solely by the power and direction of the Holy Spirit, and in that spirit of Elijah, which would precede the second coming of our Lord Jesus Christ. Our board was mainly a group of intercessors who had been part of our prayer group for some time.

We began to write (using an antiquated typewriter after having penciled many drafts on airplanes and in hotel rooms as we traveled), and our first book, *The Elijah Task*, was published in 1977. A short time later a group of men arrived at our door announcing, "God has told us to come live with you and sit at your feet!" This caused us to see how willing, eager, and presumptuous fledgling prophets could be. We tried to explain that we were certainly not yet if ever a "school" as they were interpreting our reference to "school of prophets." We visited a while and tried to be kind but firm as we told them that we had hardly arrived ourselves, and that God had not spoken a word to us of their coming. After lunch and prayer, we sent them away with direction to "study the Word, read our book, get a job" and a message to wait until "the time."

Another day a runaway arrived at our home, just to "think about" where she was going. Her brother had been in one of my classes in Mullan. We called her parents and they agreed to let her stay a while. She was with us until she graduated from high school.

A very special guest came another day: Ann B. Davis, the beloved maid, "Alice," from TV's *Brady Bunch*. We had invited her to speak at the first Women's Aglow meeting in Coeur D'Alene. She was a special blessing for our daughter Andrea, still in grade school. Andrea shared her room with Ann and took her to school with her, which of course delighted the students. When the children asked why Ann had come to town, she replied, "I came to tell people that everything the Bible says about Jesus is absolutely true!"

When *Restoring the Christian Family* and *Transformation of the Inner Man* were released, our counseling load greatly increased. Our continual cry to the Lord in prayer was "Help!" He would give us insight into people's problems, and how to pray for them. We judged the accuracy of our hearing by the Bible and the fruit in people's changed lives. We learned to recognize patterns, but disciplined ourselves not to automatically categorize people, placing them in "boxes" because they looked like others. We deliberately took breaks in busy days to rest, pray, walk, or work briefly in the garden, so we would not be inclined to see a pattern and project it onto the next several counselees, whether it applied or not.

Our intercessors prayed for us asking the Lord to keep us on His track, and we also grew as we recognized imperfections in ourselves that were similar to those in whom we ministered. When we discovered what appeared to be a new insight, we would sometimes check it out with Dr. Bill Johnson, head of the psychology department at Whitworth University, who had come to us for ministry and had become our friend.

We have never based our ministry in psychology. We have always stood on the Word of God, ministering in the Holy Spirit, always praying, and occasionally using a bit of psychology where it was relevant or helpful. This did not prevent our receiving a great deal of flak from a few self-appointed but woefully ignorant "apologists," who publicly attacked us and others in healing ministries.

When David Hunt's *The Seduction of Christianity* became available, our publisher informed us that all charismatic book sales fell to less than a third of what they had been! The book itself was the seduction of Christianity. Many people believed his mistaken concepts and slanderous charges. A number of Christian leaders and pastors attacked us publicly and forbade their people to receive us or our counselor teachers.

In dealing with David Hunt we followed Matthew 18 and contacted him to say  he had maligned us. He said that if that were so, we should send him a list of errors and false accusations. We sent him four typewritten pages or errors, misquotes, and false statements. He would not admit to any of them, except he did acknowledge putting in a wrong page number. We then phoned him to say, "You know, the Lord said that we are to know who is true and who is false by their fruits, and all these people you have attacked have borne good fruit."

He said, "John, we're not interested in fruit, only if their theology agrees with ours!" That was exactly the position of the Pharisees, who could not celebrate Jesus' miracles but could only criticize. To this day, even though many have now come to see that our ministry is biblical and much needed, many still disrespect, criticize, and slander.

But the Lord told us not to be distracted from ministry by trying to defend ourselves. To our amazement all kinds of wonderful and well-informed people like John Wimber, John White, Jack Hayford, James Robison, and Dudley Hall spoke well of us and the latter two even invited us to appear on their TV programs, telling the Christian world we had been given a bad rap.

## Some Clarifications

Though our autobiographical stories will continue to appear in the remainder of this book, this section basically ends the autobiographical part of the story of the founding of the prophetic ministry and of inner healing. I could have added many other colorful stories, such as how we were led miraculously to the house at 3657 Highland Drive in Coeur D'Alene which became the first home of Elijah House. But Paula and I have tried to capsulate our autobiographies by telling only those stories that were most formative in our lives. It was those experiences that became the raw material out of which the Lord crafted all we have taught of the prophetic and inner healing. Much that is not related here can be found in *The Elijah Task* and throughout our other books.

However, I cannot close this section of the book without clarifying a few things concerning Agnes Sanford. I did work with her for nine years, but I am not her son. She does have a son, John A. Sanford, who is also a pastor, author, teacher, and counselor. Many have been confused by the similarity.

Agnes was the first to discover how to apply the blood and cross and resurrection life of Jesus by prayer to the deep woundings and structures of the heart. She was the pioneer, the one who opened the doors of revelation for all of us who followed. Through her schools and teaching seminars around the world, she began to follow Ephesians 4:11-12 to equip the Body of Christ for ministry. She raised up a great number of disciples who have gone on to do great things for the Lord. She is deserving of much honor—and has received very little! She has become the favorite whipping girl of the misinformed apologists who arose in the 1970s and 1980s. She has been called "the voodoo woman," the "occultist who led many into witchcraft," "the modern-day heretic who has influenced many into error," and many other derogatory names.

It is time to set the record straight. She was none of those! It is important that the true facts be made known because the false smirch that has laid defiling accusations against all people involved in inner healing needs to be washed away, once and for all. The appalling thing is that none of the so-called scholars who wrote volumes against her ever came to any of us who had worked with her for years to ask if their assumptions were true. Tommy Tyson, Father Francis MacNutt, Dr. Frank Whiting, Herman Riffel, Dr. Leanne Payne, Reverend Leonard Le Poidivin, Paula and I, and a host of others could have revealed the true facts for any who would have asked. But none did.

Agnes did make some mistakes. She was a pioneer. Pioneers often stumble as they restore ancient paths of truth to walk in (see Is. 58:12). But none of her mistakes were what she has been accused of! She was not occultic. In fact, she hated anything associated with the occult. I was with her when she stomped through churches and Christian camps driving out occult things. How ironic it is, and how like the ways of the devil, to accuse her of the very thing in which she was a champion for the Lord! But again, none of her critics listened to us who could have set the record straight.

What actually happened, the mistake she made that led to the false accusations, was that she reached into other sciences and researches to try to explain the things of the Holy Spirit. I remember when she said to us, in one of our prayer and consultation times before beginning a day's teachings, "Most of the students in this School have come out of rigid negative fundamentalism into more liberal churches. Now they have come into the Holy Spirit and to our Schools to learn. Don't use the good biblical phrases; these people are so wounded by how their denominations used them that if you also use these same phrases, they'll turn you off. Reach into literature and other sciences to find ways of teaching biblical concepts, so people can hear and receive."

I remember how my spirit sank prophetically. I knew this sounded like wisdom but was wrong. I thought, *Why should we abandon the Bible to others? Why can't we just launder how we say things so that we can say everything biblically?* It was that practice of reaching into other sciences that got her into trouble.

In *The Healing Gifts of the Bible* she said, speaking of the miracles Moses wrought, "He had more occult power than the magicians of Egypt." She had studied astronomy, and in that science, the word "occult" had nothing to do with magic. It meant "when one star occludes or hides another." She only meant that the source of Moses' power was hidden from the unbelieving magicians because it was a gift from God. Later on the word "occult" metamorphosed to refer mainly or only to the forbidden practices of Deuteronomy 18:9-15.

In the same book she attempted to explain about the gifts of knowledge and perception given by the Holy Spirit. She reached into research being done at the time into paranormal phenomena, in which the terms "clairvoyance" and "clairaudience" had been coined. Those words had not then at all become connected with forbidden psychic stuff such as divination. They were merely scientific descriptive terms. So she used them. Later on, they became sullied by identification in Christians' understanding with what is occult divination. She had no such meanings in mind and would never have used such words if she had known how they would change to defile what she was saying.

Any of us who knew her could have cleared up this confusion. But the scholars who came later were shoddy in their research, and not one asked us about it. They assumed they knew what she meant and therefore what she was.

First Corinthians 2:13 says, "Which things we also speak, not in words taught by human wisdom, but in those taught by the Spirit, *combining spiritual thoughts with spiritual words*" (emphasis added). Agnes made the mistake of trying to combine spiritual thoughts with carnal or worldly words—and paid the price for it. Spiritual thoughts need to be combined with spiritual words.

But she was not guilty of occultism. That charge comes from the false scholarship of her critics.

At that time, Reverend Morton Kelsey and Agnes's son John were teaching in the School of Pastoral Care. Both had studied at the Jungian Institute in Zurich, Switzerland, and brought some of their Jungianism into the Schools. No one had yet discovered the occultism in much of Jung's experience and teachings. It seemed at first to be innocent and helpful to those involved in prayer/counseling.

Two things resulted: First, before Agnes discerned the false spirits behind Jungianism, she used some of his expressions in her teachings and incorporated some of his words in her writings. But she was never a Jungian psychologist. She had never studied it or espoused it. She merely used some of the expressions she had learned from Morton and John—again, a borrowing from other sciences to try to convey Christian concepts.

Second, after a while, she became aware, by the Holy Spirit's gifts of knowledge and discernment of spirits, that Jungianism was leading her Schools down a false path—this was long before others discerned the dangers behind Jungianism. Several times, she came to Paula and me and said, "Help me. I'm terribly worried about my boys [meaning Morton and John]. Pray for me. Pray for them." Later on, Leanne Payne became concerned about the same thing and wrote to us and joined us in praying for the cleansing of the Schools. (Eventually Leanne withdrew and formed her own "Institute of Pastoral Care.")

It should be said that later on both Morton Kelsey and John A. Sanford returned to more orthodox and biblical faith. John wrote to me and said, "You'll be happy to know that I'm returning to the faith of my mother." Whether in fact he did, I do not know; we lost track of each other. But readers need to know that Agnes' own son regarded her as a mother of truly orthodox faith who could not accept his Jungian beliefs.

Several years after these events, critics discovered those few Jungian expressions in Agnes's writings. Again, their scholarship was so shallow and incomplete that they assumed they knew what they actually did *not* know and attacked Agnes, calling her a Jungian psychologist who had corrupted many in the Church. None of those "scholars" inquired of any of us who knew the true facts, and again they falsely labeled Agnes. Unfortunately, many in the charismatic church and in the evangelical have believed the critics. This has done great damage to the ministry of the gospel of the inner man, even to this day.

Agnes pioneered her teachings at the time when old-line churches were still caught up in rationalism and intellectualism. The watchword was, "If you can explain it to me rationally, then I'll believe it." As we said earlier, that was entirely backwards, caught up in the heresy of gnosticism that elevated the mind and rationality too far—as though if we could just get our thinking right, we would be saved. We are not saved by right thinking. We are saved by the person of our Lord Jesus Christ. Again, it is ironic that Agnes was the very forerunner who called the old-line churches into faith rather than rationalistic logic, who led into faith and taught the prayer of faith that went beyond rational thinking—who also herself fell into the trap she was leading us out of!

Today, we would not attempt to explain the miraculous so anyone could believe it. We would just say, "This is what God is doing. Believe it." We no longer demand that something be explained logically before we will accept it. We use critical faculties to examine and remain sensible after we believe, but rationality is no longer the first test of whether anything spiritual is to be believed. Agnes never should have attempted to explain the gifts of knowledge and perception, much less to have reached into other sciences to explain them. No one today attempts to explain them so that people will be induced to believe. They just document events, and let the facts speak for themselves.

Here's the point: Agnes Sanford was way ahead of her time— but also way behind our time. The Body of Christ has matured in spiritual understanding and in its grasp of what the Bible says. She should have been honored for all that she discovered and revealed— but for the most part she hasn't been. Her critics examined her by the more biblically informed and accurate standards of the 1970s and 1980s, whereas she wrote and taught in the 1950s and 1960s. This would be like judging 19th-century medical practices by 21st-century standards. Her critics used unfair standards of comparison. None of her accusers have examined her fairly or accurately, according to the knowledge, practices, and standards of her day, of which she was far ahead. Had they done so, they would have accorded her the great honor she is due, rather than the slanderings they perpetrated—and that have continued to this day.

*The importance of this is that inner healing was not born in error.* As will be seen, its base is thoroughly biblical and theologically orthodox.

Critics also attacked her for what they considered to be occultic use of visualization. Many Christians have eschewed inner healing because they have thought that all of us who do it employ visualization as a main technique for healing. Both of these assumptions are false. Agnes did teach that it can be helpful to visualize what you believe God wants to accomplish in a person's life, and to describe that while praying for a person's healing. She said that such pictures give people something concrete to hold onto in faith and enable them to marshal their energies and efforts toward that goal. But that was never anything occultic. It was only common sense.

Having studied the occult, I knew what was and was not occult. For me, even what she taught was too close to what is actually occult, so I avoided it. Occultic people visualize what they want, and then pour psychic energy and practices into trying to cause that to happen. They make a mentally detailed picture of what they desire and work occult practices to make it happen. The key to discerning the difference is, "Who is doing what?" Agnes was not teaching people to make a picture. She said that we are to get our guidance from God, to find out what God wants to do, and then describe that vividly so that people can latch onto it in faith. Making up our own picture is fleshly and vulnerable to the practices of magic.

Satan copies whatever Christians can do. God creates everything by first forming the plan of what He wants to do. Hebrews 11:3 means that all things were created out of things that do not appear, just as house builders work from blueprints that were first the invisible ideas or pictures in the minds of architects. Throughout the Bible the prophets laid out the vision of what God wants and called His people into obedience to accomplish it. It was that biblical and theological realization that God often visualizes what He intends to do and then sets out to do it that was the basis of Agnes's teachings about imaginative prayer.

But I knew that many people would not hold onto the distinction that it is the Holy Spirit who is supposed to give us the picture of what God wants. Many would simply not ask God and make their own visualization, expecting God to fulfill it while employing the practices of prayer to make that picture come true. This was too close to occultic practices for me. Therefore in our teachings we have never advocated visualization. What Agnes taught was in no way occultic; it was only naive about what people following in her tracks would do.

What further complicated the issue and defiled inner healing to many was the subsequent work of Ruth Carter Stapleton. She was the sister of then-President Jimmy Carter. That notoriety catapulted her into prominence before she had sufficient time to refine her teachings or learn what was in error and correct it. She practiced much visualization and would take entire audiences on imaginary trips in which they were supposed to visualize Jesus coming to meet them on a beautiful beach (or some other restful place). Individuals in audiences were to imagine Jesus saying and doing wonderful things for them. She thought this would produce great healing experiences, and for a few it did. God responded to their faith rather than the faulty practice.

Our loving Father so wants to comfort and heal His children that occasionally He will move through our erring methods in response to our faith. Witness the numbers of miracles that happened in the early days of Christian Science. Though Mary Baker Eddy's writings were actually a recurrence of Gnostic docetic heresy, some miraculous healings have been documented in the history of Christian Science. God responded to the people's faith with His healing power, however unwise that may seem to our finite mentality. Therefore, there were a few who did receive help through Ruth Carter Stapleton's faulty practices.

Her way was erroneous for many reasons, not the least of which is that God will not allow Himself to be controlled by our making pictures of Him acting in ways we want Him to act. I know of no well-known teachers of inner healing today who teach and practice using imaginary trips or who use visualization as a primary means of accomplishing inner healing. But that did not stop critics from broad-brush, guilt-by-association libeling.

So-called scholars have attacked all inner healing and those who pray for inner healing as though we are all practitioners of visualization. This has caused many to think that visualizing is what inner healing is all about. Again none of our critical attackers have ever asked any of us what Agnes actually thought and taught or what we do or think about visualization. Let's set the record straight: Paula and I have always taught against using visualization in the ministry of inner healing. We do say that if God Himself, in the midst of our praying, gives us a picture of what He wants, to pray for that, but not to use visualization to try to make things happen.

Here is one final clarification, which is important to understand: Agnes Sanford was a healer. She wanted to heal peoples' hearts. She saw inner healing as a wonderful tool to help people find healing in their lives. The same was true of many of her disciples, notably Father Francis MacNutt, Dr. Frank Whiting, Herman Riffel, and others.

But I had been trained in a theology of transformation of character. I was the one to see and teach that what we are really doing is assisting in the work of the Holy Spirit to bring people to more and more fullness of death on the cross and resurrection into transformed lives. I saw that the Body of Christ was not maturing as it ought because so many (it may not be exaggeration to say *all*) were hung up in practices hidden in the heart that had not yet found effective death on the cross or become transformed into strengths for ministry. I saw that it was not enough to restore people to health or to functionality—people whom, at times, God did not yet intend to heal or restore—until what He intends could be fully written onto the heart (see Jer. 31:33).

We will expound on that in later chapters. For now, it is important to see that we differ from those who see the problem as the problem. Some think that if they can just remove the problem and heal wounds, they've done their task. But we say what Bob Mumford said so catchingly, "God will fix a fix to fix you. If you fix the fix God has fixed to fix you, God will just have to fix another fix to fix you!" The problem is not the problem. Problems are the crucible in which God intends to purify our character and write lessons onto our hearts so that our problems become our blessings.

The purpose of inner healing is never to erase memories or remove problems so people can function. It is to cherish all we have experienced so that out of what we have suffered we are able to minister to others (see Heb. 2:18). Our deserts are to be transformed into gardens, our degradations to glories, and all our weaknesses into strengths (see Is. 51:3).

CHAPTER EIGHT

# FOUNDING THE PROPHETIC

(JOHN)

As I testified in a previous chapter, throughout my early life I had occasionally withdrawn from my playmates in order to read about God's prophets in the Bible. At Drury University my favorite course was Rabbi Jacob's "Old Testament Prophets." Eventually I discovered that no prophets had yet arisen in our day. I grieved over the loss and saw that the Church remained lacking in strength, direction, and power because neither apostles nor prophets were in place.

Ephesians 2:19-20 says, "So then you are no longer strangers and aliens, but you are fellow citizens with the saints, and are of God's household, *having been built upon the foundation of the apostles and prophets*, Christ Jesus Himself being the corner stone" (emphasis added). I had always assumed that passage meant that two thousand years ago the apostles and prophets assisted as our Lord Jesus Christ founded the Church. But the Lord reprovingly said to me, "John, because I live today I am presently the Chief Cornerstone, and likewise apostles and prophets today are meant to be the living foundation of the Church."

I had foreseen the arising of the prophets and wrote about it in 1973-1974 in *The Elijah Task*, which was published in 1977. The book includes three sections and consequent purposes: (1) to call God's prophets to arise and learn the proper discharge of their tasks, (2) to call and teach the Body of Christ that a primary function of today's prophets is to lead into the work of intercession, and (3) to teach about the five primary and other ways of listening to God. Dan Malachuk, owner of Logos Publishers, thought *The Elijah Task* would have a very limited target audience, yet he took a chance hoping only to recoup his expenses. He actually published it solely because Agnes Sanford insisted and wrote a foreword for it, and he wanted to keep her in his stable of writers. But it fooled us all; it continues to be a best-seller 25 years later and is now regarded as a classic in its field.

### PROPHETS IN DEMAND

To my great sorrow it seemed that very few prophets were arising or learning their tasks—until John Wimber showcased the prophetic in the Denver Vineyard in 1988!

Suddenly prophets were in demand. Christians were crowding in wherever prophets were slated to appear. Paul Cain, Cindy Jacobs, Chuck Pierce, Bob Jones, John Paul Jackson, Bishop Bill Hamon, Graham Cooke, Rick Joyner, the Kansas City prophets, and a host of others were popular everywhere. Several things happened—some good, some bad.

At last prophets were arising and being recognized for who they are. Levels of faith and expectancy rose dramatically as the Lord's people came to see the reality and power of prophetic pronouncements. My teachings that prophets do exist for today were no longer a seemingly futile hollering, echoing down an empty corridor. Many scoffers were put to silence (though some diehards still want to maintain there are no prophets today despite the evidence before their eyes). Lives were impacted. Direction and purpose were restored to many.

Unbelievers were being convicted, just as Paul said, "If all prophesy, and an unbeliever or an ungifted man enters, he is convicted by all, he is called to account by all; the secrets of his heart are disclosed; and so he will fall on his face and worship God, declaring that God is certainly among you" (1 Cor. 14:24-25). Though it remains too rare that "all" prophesy accurately, many do, truly revealing "the secrets of the heart," and believers are convicted. Many prophets have arisen with such accuracy that what Paul spoke is being fulfilled today more and more often. People, both the unbelieving and

the ungifted, are being stunned out of their stupor into faith by revelations of truth in their lives.

Unfortunately, the Church was not prepared to know how to receive prophets and their words. Many began to discourteously push
their way to the front rows of meetings, hoping to be seen so as to
receive a word from a prophet. Many stopped listening to God for
themselves and implored God's prophets, unaware that their impor-
tunity could defile and turn prophets' words into divination. Most
did not comprehend how God speaks in dark speech (see Num. 12:8;
Ps. 78:2), so they misunderstood the true and deeper meanings of
what the Lord was saying.

Nor did they understand that when God prophesies high and
mighty callings, He almost always begins by humbling and purifying
His servants. Therefore circumstances most often go "in reverse"
after mighty prophecies. "My people are destroyed for lack of
knowledge." When God began to shape His servants on His potter's
wheel, preparing them to fulfill their calling, they thought their
prophecy must be false; it seemed to them to have borne only bad
fruit. Consequently, many reacted and dumped the Lord's words,
thereby failing to come into the blessed ministry God had foretold
would be theirs. In the late 1980s and on into the 1990s a widespread
backlash occurred, and suddenly prophets were no longer so widely
popular.

## SAD CONSEQUENCES OF MISUNDERSTANDING

I grieved for two reasons. First, for the damage that immaturi-
ty was causing as prophets stumbled out of darkness and secrecy into
the limelight. However, I knew that situation would only be tempo-
rary. The pattern of Church history is to discover new things and
then run off the deep end into error and embarrassment, only to
come back to balance, humbler and wiser. The Church did so with
the gift of tongues, and again when we discovered demons are real.
Suddenly, in the late 1970s and early 1980s there were demons
everywhere and vomit buckets appeared in prayer rooms—until we
came back to balance and wisdom. My grief about the prophetic was

for the hurt and disillusionment many were suffering as it seemed that some prophecies were not coming true. And, inevitably, there were errors in prophecies, presumptive words, abuses, attempts to control through the prophetic, manipulations, and confusion about whether prophets could or could not err and still be regarded as true prophets.

I have addressed these and many other issues in the book, *Elijah Among Us*, which reached the stands in June 2002, as the sequel to *The Elijah Task*. I am hoping it will settle many questions and teach the Body of Christ what prophets actually are and what they are supposed to do, which brings me to the second reason I grieved.

Prophets had been arising mainly in only one of the more than 12 major functions of their task. Many seemed to know nothing of a prophet's portfolio other than to pronounce prophetic words over individuals, groups, churches, states, and nations. I wrote *Elijah Among Us* to make the Body and its prophets aware of the magnitude and plethora of other responsibilities that pertain to the prophetic office. We'll sketch those in the next chapter. ***Suffice it to say here that the founding of the prophetic office is barely begun***. *Very few yet have caught onto the magnitude of the office or begun to grow into the fullness of its tasks.*

### THE OFFICE OF THE PROPHET VERSUS THE PROPHET OF THE MOMENT

Let's begin with some basic simple clarifications: Prophets of the moment are those who become inspired to pronounce interpretive words in meetings, usually after someone has spoken in tongues. It was of these types of prophets that Paul said, "Now I wish that you all spoke in tongues, but even more that you would prophesy; and greater is one who prophesies than one who speaks in tongues, unless he interprets, so that the church may receive edifying" (1 Cor. 14:5). A prophet of the moment is acting in a prophetic capacity, but he or she may or may not be a prophet in the office. A prophet in the office, however, is one who has been called into that position as one of the five mentioned in Ephesians 4:11, "And He gave some as apostles, and some as prophets, and some as evangelists, and some as pastors and teachers."

All five of these positions (or "offices") are gifts from God to His people, for their equipment "for the work of service, to the building up of the body of Christ" (Eph. 4:12b). Just as a priest (or pastor) is set aside to be a priest forever, after the order of Melchizedek—"For it is witnessed of Him, Thou art a priest forever according to the order of Melchizedek" (Heb. 7:17)—each person in those offices is also set aside to be so forever. The Lord may elevate an individual to more than one office, but that person does not abdicate his former office; he simply wears another hat.

The task of a prophet of the moment is accomplished once his word has been said. He has no more or less responsibility for it than any other. On the other hand, a prophet in the office cannot take off the prophetic mantle. He wears it 24 hours a day, 365 days a year. He or she is on call, like a minuteman in American revolutionary days, enlisted to respond wherever and whenever satan's forces appear. A prophet in the office is called upon to judge what prophets of the moment and other prophets say: "And let two or three prophets speak, and let the others *pass judgment*" (1 Cor. 14:29, emphasis added), which requires gifts of discernment and wisdom and is fraught with responsibility for the sanctity and safety of the congregation.

## DO PROPHETS ALWAYS KNOW THE FUTURE?

Some think that prophets are those who act as seers, talking about the future all the time, or as gifted people who know and reveal hidden and secret things, as Samuel knew about Saul's donkeys and the groups of men who would meet Saul along the way. Some people also think that prophets always know or understand what is happening. Though it is true that occasionally God does reveal future and hidden things through His prophets, that ability is not who they are or what they do primarily. Nor do they always know about details or the meaning of what is going on.

When the Shunammite woman frantically rushed to the man of God and fell at his feet because her son had died, Gehazi the servant would have pushed her away, but Elisha said, "Let her alone, for her soul is troubled within her; and *the Lord has hidden it from me and has not told me*" (2 Kings 4:27b, emphasis added). Prophets speak whatever the Lord tells them to speak—past, present, or future, known or unknown. Since God doesn't always tell them or they don't always listen or do so accurately, they don't always know or understand what is happening.

Amos 3:7 says, "Surely the Lord God does nothing unless He reveals His secret counsel to His servants the prophets." From this Scripture some have erroneously deduced that a true prophet will always know everything about everything. And if he doesn't, he must not be a true prophet of the Lord. But we need to learn to read God's Word circumspectly so as not to add our interpretations and then think He said what we think. This text does not say that prophets know everything. It says God reveals His secret counsel concerning what He is doing, not necessarily every detail of what He is doing. Nor does it say that He reveals everything *before* He does it, only that He reveals His secret counsel *about* what He does.

We do a lot of things apart from God, and God may or may not reveal to His prophets those things that people have done or will do. Those things are not what Amos was talking about. He said God reveals His counsel *about what **He** is doing*. So, prophets may be given the ability to understand why God does things, and what they mean, without knowing beforehand what events will happen; or by revelation afterwards concerning what has already happened. And they may be as ignorant as anyone else about the myriad of incidents that will happen or have happened in our daily lives apart from what God is doing. If they know, it is because God has chosen to reveal; but He doesn't always reveal. When God acts, He reveals His secret counsel about what He is doing, but He does not always reveal what He is doing or the myriad of things men and women do in which He is not acting.

It is important to comprehend this Scripture because many people have gone to recognized prophets thinking that those prophets ought always to have a word for them. I fear for the people who expect and demand words from prophets as though they were some kind of coin vending machine that should pop out a word every time a coin of demand is put into their slot. And I worry about prophets who can rattle off prophecies on demand one after the other, and think they should. Prophecy can quickly turn to presumption and divination. God doesn't always speak, and prophets and people need to know and respect that fact.

## PROPHETS AND DREAMS AND VISIONS

Much teaching and clarification is given about dreams and visions in both *The Elijah Task* and *Elijah Among Us*, in Bishop Bill Hamon's books and his daughter-in-law's valuable book about dreams and visions, and in the writings of many others, notably Ernest B. Gentile and Rick Joyner. The discussion of them here is to clarify some issues concerning principles and common errors.

Among the five primary ways God speaks—which are listed in Numbers 12—dreams, visions, and dark speech are the three in which God speaks in parables, symbols, and signs, precisely to cause us to ponder humbly rather than jump to conclusions. Hearing accurately is difficult for many reasons, perhaps the most common being the interference of our flesh, most often through our unregenerate mind (see Rom. 8:5-7). One basic reason God employs dreams and visions is to bypass the interference of our minds. The simple difference between dreams and visions is that dreams happen while we are asleep, when the mind is least able to interfere; whereas, during visions we are awake, but our mind is not as capable of interfering as it would be if we were listening to spoken words. In both dreams and visions, pictures require pondering for interpretation, which is what God wants, even as "Mary treasured up all these things, pondering them in her heart" (Lk. 2:19).

From this knowledge of dreams and visions comes several bits of teaching and advice: First, know that in God's economy He can use dreams and visions to implant cautions and thoughts in our hearts for many levels of meaning and for many subsequent events. *There is seldom only one meaning to a dream*, and seldom does one event exhaust the possible import for many subsequent events. In other words, beware of thinking that one interpretation is all there is to any dream or vision, and that any dream or vision may be about only one event.

Many examples are provided in our two prophetic books, one of which is a man dreamed of getting into bed with a woman who was not his wife. He was horrified, fearful that he was being warned of a possible affair. That idea is a possible meaning and ought to call for caution and cleansing of the heart, plus strengthening one's marriage relationship. But that may not be the only meaning. If it is to be taken personally, the Holy Spirit may be warning that his spirit (the man himself in the dream) may be about to "get in bed" with a wrong theology, or erroneous way of thinking, or bad practice in business or relationships. The woman in the dream can be symbolic of anything he ought not to be involved in or with.

Dreams and visions can be interior and/or exterior, so his dream can also be about someone else or some situation about which the Lord is calling him to ponder and pray for. Someone else may be in danger of having an affair, in which case the dream is not about him though it seems to be. We are one with others; their life is our concern, and their sin can be portrayed by the Holy Spirit as though it were our own, because in spiritual fact we are one and their trouble is as our own. Or someone or some group may be in danger of being tempted into something inappropriate. The dream calls one into pondering and praying, waiting for the Lord to give other clues for more specific applications.

This way God has of speaking to us in ambiguous, dark, or figurative speech leaves us with anxiety and thus to vulnerability to want to find answers—perhaps too quickly and thus erroneously. God's way of speaking so indirectly through dreams, visions, and dark speech calls us into the faithful posture of waiting patiently upon Him. Often we are too impatient, and we miss the imports and signals God would reveal further along the way—even as the Israelites jumped to conclusions and missed the true import of so many of the meanings of visions and prophecies that foretold our Lord's coming.

What are we supposed to do? Don't get isolated. Confer humbly with brothers and sisters. Pray for revelation(s). Don't think one event or meaning alone has completed God's purpose for your dream or vision. Stay alert. Remain in pondering and prayer.

This doesn't mean that you should always have your head in the clouds, pondering so much of the time that you miss people and events that are happening practically all around you. It means that you should keep things simmering on the back burner of your consciousness so that God can leap meanings to your renewed mind whenever He chooses to add a piece of understanding to your ongoing puzzles.

If you are a prophet, beware of being coerced or encouraged to offer a definitive meaning for someone's dream or vision. Offer suggestions of possible meanings to aid in the other's pondering. What good would it do if God gives a dream to someone to cause a time of faithful pondering, and then you preempt His purposes by blatting out a meaning that shuts down His intended time of pondering and praying? If you have a dream and go to prophets for interpretation, value what they tell you, but don't shut down your own questing. Continue to think and pray. God can reveal His meaning(s) when actions are necessary if your heart is right. Dreams and visions call us to set our heart right, so that we are prepared to walk into understanding and actions relevant to what He is revealing.

## Be Willing to Wait

A basic principle of walking in the prophetic is the painful art of humble waiting and enduring the jagged edges of possibilities, trusting the God of providence and mystery to make things clear when He is prepared to do so. Most prophetic errors occur when we get in a hurry to remove the anxiety from our lives by finding definitive answers, when at the same time God may not be ready to make things that clear. Some people think that a prophet's major function is to remove the tension of not knowing by revealing God's purposes and plans. It is easy to see why people think that way because sometimes that is precisely God's intention for sending His prophet. But remember that God reveals His plans and purposes when He is ready to bring clarity to situations over which our pondering time has already prepared us to receive definitive answers.

Prophets are not know-it-alls who are here just so that people don't have to live with the unanswered questions of dreams and visions—or in any aspect of daily life. Prophets are those servants whom God may use to confirm things to us when our pondering and praying about our own dreams and visions are complete—or to present to us those revelatory dreams and visions they have seen that set us into requisite times of pondering and praying, and consequent revelation.

And we need to remember that when pondering and praying have made it possible to respond appropriately to a summons from God in one or two instances, our dream or vision may also have many other possible purposes in God's economy. This does not mean that we should have our noses stuck to the grindstone of dream journals all the time, afraid we'll miss some vast purpose God has for us if we don't; but that we should file our dreams into the active recall section of our mind, remaining alert, so that the Holy Spirit can remind us of them when something of significance happens. In the Bible, Peter said that He would make it possible for His followers to recall what they needed to when times would demand (see 2 Pet. 1:12-15, especially verse 15). The Holy Spirit is able to recall dreams, visions, and meanings to our minds when we need them.

I'll close this section by repeating a story told in *Elijah Among Us*. There was a mother who kept having a dream of a boy lying face down in a pool of water. She pondered and prayed about it for several days. Then one evening she suddenly threw her dish towel down and ran across several neighboring yards—and plucked her son from drowning in a neighbor's pond!

Do you suppose that was the only meaning to her dream? Could it be that there are many situations in which people could be in danger of "drowning," "face down," meaning, without seeing what the problem is? We can drown emotionally, spiritually, in marriage and other relationships, in business, and many other ways. If she continues to ponder and pray, not thinking that one incident exhausted God's purposes in her dream, is it possible God might use her to save a number of people from many situations?

## RECOGNIZING A PROPHET'S CALLING

No prophet becomes a prophet by his or her own choice. The office is not elective. Nor does a decision to become a prophet, coupled with study and practice, however valuable the discipline and the learning, call or confirm. Gifting in prophetic abilities may indicate that God may be calling but is not in itself the calling or validation that a person is a prophet. The desires of individuals, groups, and churches do not suffice as a call. Prophetic words from established prophets that a person is called to be a prophet are valuable and to be heeded, but if confirming words do not follow, those words are only presumptive, for "every fact is to be confirmed by the testimony of two or three witnesses" (2 Cor. 13:1b). Even so, two or three witnesses may be just as presumptive or erroneous as one alone. Therefore, calls to the prophetic office need to be followed not only by confirming words but also signs.

What are the signs that confirm a calling to the prophetic office? Operating in prophetic gifts is a sign of prophetic calling but in itself is not sufficient. Satan and the occultly adept can mimic most prophetic giftings for a while, even as the magicians could ape the first signs Moses wrought before the Pharaoh. Prophetic pronouncements that reveal secrets of the heart are not sufficient signs of true calling. Psychics on "900" phone lines can do that almost as well as the Lord's prophets!

Boldness to confront sin is no sign; it takes little or no prophetic gifting to recognize sin, and certainly no calling to confront— flesh can do that. I saw one lady, who thought she had a prophetic gift of discernment and ability to confront, operate as a Jezebel in a demonic gift of accusation through which she tore an entire church apart while her Ahab-like husband did nothing to stop her rampages!

She was most certainly not a prophet of the Lord, though she thought her "gifting" proved she was.

*Strikingly, the most telling confirming sign of a prophet's calling is when the Lord begins to test and crush that person!*

## A PROPHET'S TRAINING

Prophets are trained in two ways. First, under the "green tree." In biblical days, established prophets taught fledgling prophets literally under "green trees." The green tree was much like our modern-day banyan tree, which sends out limbs from which trailers descend that in turn root into the ground and become supportive and feeding trunks. Green trees can expand over large areas, even as a banyan tree in Lahaina on Maui has filled an entire small city block. People thought such trees were a tree of heaven, planted by God, and cared for by Him alone. Some think that "the shadow of the Almighty" in Psalm 91:1 may be an oblique reference to the sense of God's protection under the shade of a green tree. In the safety and cool shade of such trees, prophets in biblical times taught learners the facts and methods of the office, by question and answer. Today, there are few "green trees" for beginning prophets. Bishop Bill Hamon conducts such a school at his place near Tallahassee, Florida. But such training is not confirmation of a prophetic call; it follows upon confirmation.

Secondly, prophets are trained by being humiliated and crushed by the Holy Spirit (see Mt. 21:44). Gifting, serving in prophetic ways, prophetic words calling into the office, study and practice may be partial indications. All together, they comprise a rather convincing testimony of the veracity of a calling. But wisdom dictates waiting to see how the Lord begins to work in a person's life before deciding irrevocably that a person is truly a prophet.

If sufferings, disappointments, persecutions, unanswered prayers, and frustrations begin to pile up—watch. If the fledgling persists in faith and humbly receives the crushing, most likely a prophet is being formed on the Potter's wheel. *In the end, it is character that is the most telling sign of a true prophet.*

The crushing should eventuate in a gentle and humble servant who will do nothing to hurt, force, or manipulate another. Prophets who demand and control, impervious to the Spirit's signals for sensitivity to the thoughts and feelings of others, are either immature or not prophets at all, and are actually wolves in sheep's clothing.

## THE POSITION OF PROPHETS

Among the fivefold ministry, apostles, prophets, evangelists, and teachers may be local and/or extra-local—pastors are the only servants who are by definition local at all times and in all cases. They are as the Lord's sergeants who run His army day by day in intimate contact with His people. If the first three could be considered as higher officers, it needs to be remembered that in our Lord's seemingly upside-down ways, the lowest are as the highest and the highest as the lowest. My belief is that all the other four ministries serve the pastors.

My teaching is that prophets need to place themselves under the authority of the local pastor and elders in every church and city they enter. I will not give a word in a local church without first informing the pastor and giving him and his elders the right to judge that word. *After I leave, he is the one who will have to live with whatever I have deposited.* If he says he thinks that word is not for his congregation, I will not outrank him and present it anyway. I will not give that word. I have performed my duty (as in Ezekiel 33), and the blood is now upon the pastor. If it was a true word and the pastor allowed it, his people are blessed. If it was a true word and the pastor and elders disallowed it, the blood is on their heads.

A true prophet's calling can also be discerned by this matter of humble protocol: *One who overrides local authority is either not a prophet, a false prophet, or an immature prophet.*

In my writing thus far, it may be determined correctly that I am advising the Body of Christ not to be hasty in assuming that a person is truly called or trained to be a prophet. Our Lord is never in a hurry. Instead of inappropriately and rashly honoring a man or woman as though prophetic status were already confirmed, there is time to reserve judgment, to accumulate the facts of history, and to wait for many confirming signs.

God places the burden of determining a true prophet where it belongs—on *us*, to "test the spirits to see whether they are from God..." (1 Jn. 4:1b). God Himself tells us in Deuteronomy 13:1-5 that dreamers or prophets may arise and give false words. But note, He said that if the prophet's sign or wonder comes true (see Deut. 13:2), and he leads people after other gods, you shall not listen to him and shall put him to death (see Deut. 13:5). The prophet's word was true; it was his teaching that was in error. But God uses these things to test us, to know whether we will love and follow *Him* rather than His servants idolatrously (see Deut. 13:3-4).

## TRUE PROPHETS CAN MAKE MISTAKES AND GIVE FALSE WORDS

Two erroneous teachings about the prophetic have gripped the minds of many: first, that a true prophet never errs in what he says; and second, that if he does, he is to be put to death, by God if not by us. Readers can find a fuller exposition of this subject in the first chapter of *Elijah Among Us*. Suffice it to say here that whatever we believe, about any spiritual subject, ought to be scripturally justifiable, or be rejected. Jeremiah 23 and Ezekiel 13 castigated prophets who were erring, but nothing is said of putting them to death. In the day of Jehoshaphat, he and the king of Israel called for the prophet Micaiah to come and give them a word. Many other prophets had prophesied that God would give them victory over the king of Syria. But Micaiah foretold the true word that they would be defeated and the king of Israel would be killed (see 1 Kings 22). *However, none of the erring prophets were put to death.*

Nor were they, in this instance or in Jeremiah 23 and Ezekiel 13, called false prophets, only erroneous in what they were doing. It was not said that they were not real prophets of the Lord, though their words on those occasions were wrong. Perhaps the appellation "false" should properly be reserved for those who have no intention to be true, who are using the title for some base or false motive. On the other hand, true prophets who make even a number of errors are not false; contrarily, they are immature, poorly instructed, or just plain dumb. Balaam became a false prophet and would have been put to death had not his donkey sighted the angel of death and shied away—but note, even the false prophet Balaam was spared and not put to death.

Hananiah, in Jeremiah 28:17, was put to death, as were some others on various occasions. But Hananiah was put to death because he "taught rebellion." It does not sanctify the merciful and kind nature of our Father and our Savior and Lord to portray God as a tyrant with a huge fly swatter who smashes prophets who make slight mistakes. Who would want to serve such a master? Death was reserved only for those who made grievously harmful mistakes or for those who intended, as Balaam did, to be false—and then only if lack of sufficient repentance prevented grace.

## No One Should Want to Be a Prophet

Even though we have such a wonderful, kind, and gracious Lord, no one in His right mind should want to be a prophet! The responsibilities are too great, and the consequences so drastic.

On the evening before the beginning of the great Sunshine Mine fire that killed 91 men, I had been playing basketball with Marvin Chase, a friend of mine, in his backyard. As I drove away, the Lord said, "There is a fire in the Sunshine Mine. Go back and warn Marvin," who was the superintendent of the Sunshine Mine near Kellogg, Idaho.

I thought, *How can there be a fire in a rock mine? That's crazy. I must not be hearing God.* So I didn't go back. I learned later that Marvin would have honored me and gone to check and would have found the fire just beginning to burst from smoldering into flames. Oil had soaked into wooden rail ties and spontaneous combustion broke out among some rags that had been thrown aside. For days I staggered around under a load of guilt. Ninety-one men died because I disobeyed the express command of the Lord!

Less dramatic than that but not less impacting upon those of us who are prophets is the fact that the words we bring can drastically alter the lives of people to whom we bring words. Knowing that tragedies are coming and that their prevention or alleviation depends upon the successful calling of Christians to respond in prayers of repentance weighs heavily on us. Even prophesying blessings, like a marriage or a pregnancy or some other good thing coming, is frightening because the Lord's prophet is assailed by fears that his word may be presumptive or in error—until it happens. And the good thing may not happen because many prophecies are conditional and dependent upon proper responses by the people, who may not react accordingly.

When blessings don't come people seldom look to their own failings for the reason. More often they say things like, "That was a false prophecy!" or worse yet, "That was a false prophet's word!" Given mankind's sinful nature and propensity to cast blame anywhere than on the self, the prophetic is a tough place to be.

Furthermore, many people don't want to be warned of trouble coming, especially if it has been caused by their sinful behavior, so they may look for anything for which to blame or slander the prophet so they don't have to listen. The prophet's walk is therefore deeply lonely, even if he has learned to be corporate and allows others to share the burdens. "Nobody knows the troubles I've seen" is fully understood by prophets.

On the other hand, closeness with our Lord Jesus and Father God is its own inestimable reward. Even though earthly rewards of joy and satisfaction do come, as the prophet sees his efforts blessing the lives of many, they pale in comparison to the joy that awaits him or her in the treasures of reward laid up for him in Heaven.

CHAPTER NINE

# TWELVE MAJOR FUNCTIONS OF THE PROPHET

(JOHN)

Many of the historic functions of the prophetic office have not yet been rediscovered and activated. It is our hope that as the Body of Christ, especially the Lord's prophets, read *Elijah Among Us* and this book, many will take hold of the potentialities of the office and begin more fully to express them. The functions of the prophetic office are as many and varied as the mind of the Lord is high above us! Though I will speak here of only 12 specific functions, no one has yet begun to tap into the vast reservoir of the Lord's possibilities. I say this at the outset lest the list seem to comprise all there is to the office. Our Lord is about to open new vistas of exploration, experience, and service not only to the Body but to the whole world. We need to be alert, flexible, and obedient to move into what God has long planned for the Church and the world.

Not all prophets are called to—or are capable of—moving in all the possibilities of the office. In fact, I know of none who are. God calls each prophet into his or her own unique portfolio. As each serves well in what is given, our Lord delights to say, "Well done, thou good and faithful servant," and opens new areas and consequent anointing and gifting. God calls and equips us to be specialists, fitting us together with others until "every joint supplies" (see Eph. 4:16) and all move together in His service to accomplish what only a group or an army is able to do.

This chapter explains prophetic functions and includes some godly parameters to live by. To provide easy reference, following are the 12 major functions of a prophet:

1. Blessing.
    A. Pronounce blessing.
    B. Enable God's blessings.

2.    Healing.

3.    Pronounce judgment.

4.    Warn of impending judgment or tragedy.

5.    Protect or rescue.

6.    Give direction, guidance, or confirmation.

7.    Rebuke, reprove, or correct.

8.    Edify, teach, and interpret dreams and visions.

9.    Equip the saints for ministry.

10.    Work for unity.

11.    Call for intercession and repentance.

12.    Express and model God's love in Christ.

### Blessing—Pronounce Blessing

There are many examples from the Bible in which a prophet pronounced blessing. In Second Kings 4:8-17 there was a Shunammite woman who perceived that Elisha, who often passed by, was a prophet. She mentioned to her husband that it would be well to prepare an upper room with a bed, a chair, and table for him. They did so, and Elisha came to stay there. That meant that Elisha was duty bound to bless her. Calling Gehazi, his servant, he asked what his hostess needed. Gehazi reminded him that she had no son. So Elisha said to call her, and when she came, he pronounced that by the same time next year she would embrace a son. The blessing happened as he said it would.

In Second Kings 4:1-7 a widow complained to Elisha that creditors were coming to take away her two children. Elisha told her to gather every jar and pot she could find and pour oil into them. The miracle of increase did not stop until no more empty vessels could be found. Elisha told her to sell the oil, pay her debts, and live off the bountiful remainder.

In Israel there were three kinds of beggars. The first were real beggars. People gave to them because of kindness and because they knew God would reward them for giving.

The second type were not beggars for money, but were people who suffered from an incurable disease, who had exhausted every kind of medical help to no avail. These went to roadsides or the temple to sit and beg. Like blind Bartimaeus, they may actually have been wealthy. (See the stories in *The Elijah Task* and *Elijah Among Us* for full expositions.) They begged in order to humble themselves before the Lord, hoping that a holy man would come by and God would have mercy and heal them. For this reason Bartimaeus would not be silent and cried out all the more when passersby tried to silence him—this was the very opportunity he had been waiting for! (See Mark 10:46-52.) Most likely this is why the man lame from birth was begging beside the temple gate, hoping for healing—which Peter and John pronounced! (See Acts 3:1-10.)

The third type of beggar was not a beggar in the real sense, but one sent out without two tunics or sandals, food or money for lodging, as Jesus did His disciples (see Lk. 10:4). God purposefully made His prophets dependent upon provision from His people because that would enable Him to bless the people with a prophet's reward, as He said in Matthew 10:40-42. (Again, full exposition of this subject can be found in *Elijah Among Us*.) Prophets today are still gifts from God for the people, sent out without their own provisions, made dependent upon the people's generosity, so that God may have opportunity to bless those who give to His servants.

For this reason, no prophet should demand an honorarium as a requirement for his coming. A true prophet comes and goes wherever God sends, not where money beckons. Never should he or she ask for money or any other kind of gift as a condition for coming and serving. If he does, he is either immature, uninformed, or downright greedy and thus false to his calling. On the other hand, woe betide those who announce that "this evening's offering will go entirely to the prophet" and then give a meager portion or none at all and keep the money for their church or themselves. They have not only committed the same sin for which Ananias and Sapphira were slain by the Holy Spirit, but they have also robbed themselves and their people of the blessings God could have given them had they given as they should have to the Lord's prophet.

It is one of a prophet's greatest joys to be allowed to pronounce God's blessings upon His people.

### BLESSING—ENABLE GOD'S BLESSINGS

The primary way prophets enable God's blessings is to pronounce blessing, but there are other ways God can bring blessings through His prophets. When revelations about who and what needs prayer are coming forth from many people at a prayer meeting, we have observed that everyone else's anointing and gifting are enhanced when prophets are present. Their mere presence and example enables and emboldens.

Many times I have seen the prospective spouses of Christians, long before they have met them. I won't describe what they look like, but telling them that their mate does exist enables faith and hope— and countless times that wife or husband has shown up, appearing exactly as seen. I have seen babies before their conception, and though usually I won't say what the sex is or what the child looks like, faith and hope are encouraged, and the blessing happens. Sometimes I have not been led to speak of the blessing of a coming marriage or child I have seen, and have only prayed—thus blessing was enabled without a spoken word.

I, and other prophets, have silently prayed blessings on businesses, farms, churches, and families, and what we have seen and called for has happened. Thus we have enabled blessings without speaking words aloud about them. For this reason Israelite families urged prophets to stay with them, hoping to be rewarded with blessings from God. That is still so today. Memory can't recall how many times people have phoned us to relate with joy the strings of blessings that have happened in their family after we visited. It was not that we did anything or deserved any credit; it was simply that God was enabled to bless because people gave hospitality or other good things to His servants the prophets, and God wanted to bless them in return.

## HEALING

Examples of healing abound in the Old Testament, and the New. When the Shunammite's son grew old enough, he went out to be with his father in the field. Medical science today probably would say he had a sunstroke. The youth lay in his mother's lap a while and then died. Elisha raised him to life again (see 2 Kings 4:18-37).

In Genesis 20 when King Abimelech had believed Abraham's half-lie and took Sarah into his household, *intending* to go to bed with her, all the wombs of his household were closed. God spoke to him in mercy, kept him from sinning with her, and told him to go to Abraham "...for he is a prophet, and he will pray for you, and you will live" (Gen. 20:7a). "And Abraham prayed to God; and God healed Abimelech and his wife and his maids, so that they bore children. For the Lord had closed fast all the wombs of the household of Abimelech because of Sarah, Abraham's wife" (Gen. 20:17-18).

Incidentally, note that when the heathen King Abimelech only intended to sin with Sarah, all his people's wombs were closed! Today there is a foolish belief propounded by many that what our President does sexually doesn't matter so long as it "doesn't interfere with the performance of his duties as President." One function of prophets today is to revive in all of us a true corporate conscience, that whatever we do affects all because we are, in deed and fact, corporate. When our President sinned sexually, that opened vast doors to destruction of morality and to dissolution of families throughout the land!

Other examples of healings include: Elisha healed the food when gatherers mistakenly included poisonous gourds (see 2 Kings 4:38-41). Isaiah told King Hezekiah he would die; but when the king turned his face to the wall and repented, the Lord spoke to Isaiah before he left the palace, sending him back—and God healed Hezekiah (see 2 Kings 20:11). Peter and John healed the man lame from birth (see Acts 3: 1-10).

There isn't enough space here to tell of the many other miracles of healing throughout the New Testament. Suffice it to say that there is plenty of evidence that healing was, and remains, a major function of God's prophets.

## PRONOUNCE JUDGMENT

Jeremiah pronounced judgment upon Pashur, whose name meant "peace," declared his name to be changed to Magormissabib, which means "terror all around," and informed him that he would see death and destruction upon all he loved (see Jer. 20:3-5). Jeremiah also pronounced judgment on Hananiah that he would die before the year's end (see Jer. 28:15-17). In the New Testament, Peter pronounced death upon Ananias and Sapphira for lying to the Holy Spirit (see Acts 5:1-11).

Prophets today are still commanded—rarely, thank God—to pronounce His judgments on people's lives. No prophet who *wants* to pronounce judgments is a true prophet. I have been required to do so only a very few times, and did so only after great soul searching and repentance before God that my own heart be as His. Thus, one of the reasons servants should be reluctant to become prophets—the burden is too heavy.

## WARN OF IMPENDING JUDGMENT OR TRAGEDY

When God *pronounces* judgment, it is too late for anything but the most fervent repentance to avert disaster. But God warns of judgments and tragedies precisely because He doesn't want them to happen. He knows that if His people will respond in repentance and prayer, He can prevent judgments and tragedies, and for that reason speaks warnings through His prophets.

In the reign of good King Josiah, the book of the law was found while the temple was being cleansed. Josiah sent to ask Huldah the prophetess about the book. Huldah warned of great destruction coming because the people had turned from God's Word to all manner of evils. Josiah called the people into repentance and Huldah announced that the evils would not come in his time. Josiah, not content that his people would suffer after his time, instituted many reforms and tore down the altars of the Baalim. Because Josiah responded, tragedy was averted (see 2 Kings 22).

Indeed, most of us as children are taught of another famous example when people heeded a prophet's warning and God spared them from disaster. Jonah was sent to prophesy destruction upon Nineveh. However, the king declared a time of fasting and repenting in sackcloth and ashes; and because the people repented, Nineveh was not destroyed.

Today, prophets exercise the same function. Readers can find many stories and examples of prophetic warnings in *The Elijah Task* and *Elijah Among Us*, in Bishop Bill Hamon's books, and those of Cindy Jacobs, and many other authors. Prophets give warnings to rescue nations, states, churches, groups, and individuals, concerning large issues and small. God is interested in every detail of our lives.

## PROTECT OR RESCUE

While God may protect and rescue His people through warnings of judgment, He also calls His prophets to protect or rescue His people when sin and judgments are not involved. Elisha warned the king of Israel each time the king of Syria would set traps for him, until the Syrian king cried out "Which of us is for the king of Israel?" (2 Kings 6:11b). He thought there was a traitor among them. When an advisor informed him it was not a traitor but the prophet Elisha, he sent an army to capture Elisha. You probably know the rest of the story. Gehazi awoke terrified to find 100,000 warriors encamped on their doorstep, but Elisha unafraid said, "Open his eyes, Lord," and behold there was an army of chariots of fire upon the mountains encircling all! Elisha struck the army blind, led them to his king, and advised that the army be sent home humbled and humiliated—and there was no more trouble with Syria. So Elisha, his king, and all of Israel were rescued from harm.

While I was in the pastorate there was not a death or an accident among our people that the Lord had not called me into prayer about before they happened! Bad deaths were often averted, good ones bathed in prayer. Many accidents were either completely prevented or miraculously prevented from causing serious harm. Think how marvelous it would be if the Lord were to raise up in every church prophets to whom He could call so that tragedies could be prevented. How many young people have died needlessly because the foundations of the Church are not in place? How many deaths could have been averted if enough prophets had been on station, alert to the summons of the Lord?

### GIVE DIRECTION, GUIDANCE, OR CONFIRMATION

Most of the prophets who have arisen in our time go about giving words of direction, guidance, and confirmation to individuals, groups, churches, states, nations, etc. This is the function most Christians are aware of, both among prophets and recipients of personal words. These words can be very valuable, and often are. They certainly were in biblical times.

Often kings and their counselors came to prophets asking for guidance, "Shall we go up against the enemy? Will He give us victory? Will He march with our armies?" The Lord told David to go up "when you hear the sound of marching in the tops of the balsum trees" and God would give him victory (see 2 Kings 5:24; 1 Chron. 14:15). He did, and God did.

Samuel told Saul that his asses had been found and that he would meet two and then three men who would be as signs to him (see 1 Sam. 10), and precisely that happened.

Prophets in Antioch confirmed God's call upon Barnabas and Saul to become His apostles to the Gentiles (see Acts 13:1-4).

Simeon and Anna confirmed to the wondering hearts and minds of Joseph and Mary that their Son was indeed the promised Messiah, and more (see Lk. 2:22-35, 36-38).

So, personal prophetic words are both scriptural and valuable, often extremely so. As I testified in *Elijah Among Us*, a word from Sandy De Loach drastically changed the course of our ministry, calling us into reconciliatory work among natives and whites the world over. Personal words said by many at the first Apostolic Council of Prophetic Elders called C. Peter Wagner into apostleship, and other prophetic words launched him into forming the Wagner Institute. Words given by Jim Goll, Jim Recard, and Mickey Robinson at a

Healing Rooms conference in Spokane not only broadened the scope of our ministry but proclaimed a Holy Spirit-inspired union between the prophetic and healing, especially inner, and opened vast gates of ministry in the Northwest.

Most people in the charismatic movement could share testimonies of being greatly impacted by prophetic words. But great blessings seldom come without possibility of equal harm. Words are sometimes presumptive, erroneous, or just out of proper perspective in the Lord's timing. Many people have not known how to respond to prophetic words and have rushed into unsanctified decisions and actions. Many have not understood that God often speaks figuratively even when He seems to be speaking clearly and directly.

The Body of Christ is only slowly maturing with regard to hearing and responding to prophets and their words. We wrote *Elijah Among Us* in order to correct the problem of misunderstanding the import of prophetic words, and to instruct the Church how to understand and respond to prophets. Whoever desires to obey the Lord's calling in these days should study to become a workman who needs not to be ashamed, devouring first the Bible and then the writings of such people as Bishop Bill Hamon, Jim Goll, Ernest Gentile, Cindy Jacobs, myself, and others.

### REBUKE, REPROVE, OR CORRECT

The most egregious example of a prophet's rebuke in the Old Testament, perhaps in all of history, occurred when Elijah stood against the idolatry that had become increasingly offensive to the Lord in Israel. Calling for a gathering on Mount Carmel, he set up a showdown between the prophets of Baal and the Lord. Elijah rebuked the people for going "hesitating between two opinions" (see 1 Kings 18, verse 21 especially). He called down fire on a bullock soaked with water and then killed 450 prophets of Baal and 400 prophets of Asherah.

Nathan rebuked King David for his secret sin with Bathsheba (see 2 Sam. 12). In the way he reproved David, he laid down a model for all subsequent prophets to follow. In the Way of our Lord, Old or

New, truth is not merely accurate facts. Truth has become, for us, the nature of God. One can receive a true word of rebuke or correction, but if it is given arrogantly or insensitively, that word becomes false because it does not sanctify the loving nature of our Lord Jesus Christ who is the way, the truth, and the life (John 14:6). Nathan invited David to judge a hypothetical case, and then revealed that David was himself the man he had judged. Nathan's gentle wisdom invited David into the process of revelation and repentance rather than imperiously dumping a load of accusation upon him.

Today, God is raising up Nathanic prophets. He wants to grant His erring children opportunity to repent and confess, so that as much of His mercy as possible can be  allowed. All prayer counselors, whether they be prophets or not, act in a prophetic Nathanic function when they help people to see their hidden sins and sin natures, so that they can repent and find death on the cross and freedom in Christ. How wonderful it would be if there were prophets in every church who could be trusted by God to see the hidden sins and sin nature of the members so that God could bring redemption into each circumstance before it could mount to tragedy! My prophetic word to the Church is that precisely that scenario will happen. It already is in too rare instances, but it will become commonplace, a habit of life in God's redeemed and redeeming Church.

What if this role of prophets could be expanded into the marketplace? Perhaps the scandals now reverberating through the economic community, set off by Enron, would never have grown to threaten economic stability in our time. I was told beforehand by the Lord that great scandals would be revealed which "could bring down our entire economy," but whom could I tell? To date, the secular world does not listen to us. What if prophets were again received, as in Old Testament days, by political and economic leadership?

I knew by prophetic revelation what John F. Kennedy and later Bill Clinton were doing sexually while they were in office, and of the great harm that was spreading through America, but to whom could I have spoken? Who would have listened, or had the power to do anything about it?

Two years before John F. Kennedy was assassinated, I saw the entire assassination by a vision, but who would have heard had I tried to warn him? (Actually I did send a warning, by a letter addressed to the Secret Service, but I never knew if it had even been received.) Though this testimony properly belongs in the previous section regarding warnings before tragedies, I include it here because it is an illustration of the present lack of access of prophets to speak rebuke or give warnings. That will change. Another prophetic word I present here is that the day will come when political and economic leaders will have the wisdom and courage to call upon the Lord's prophets—rather than to psychic seers and other false guides to whom some have turned.

### Edify, Teach, and Interpret Dreams and Visions

First Corinthians 14:1-5 informs us that a major purpose and function of prophets today is to edify the Church. All that prophets do is to be judged by that criterion. Did their word edify? Did the rebuke come exemplifying Jesus' nature so that that fact itself edified the Church? Did their foretelling only frighten or falsely exalt, or did it also edify? Even in the pronouncing of stern judgment, was the manner of it edifying to all?

What does it mean to edify? I think it means to educate, to inform, and to model the nature of our gentle Lord, to sanctify His nature before the eyes of mankind.

Teaching is therefore a major function of prophets. If a prophet does all the prophesying, interpreting of dreams and visions, interceding and warning, etc., he has failed as a prophet. His job is to work himself out of a job by raising up others in their own gifting.

Having and interpreting dreams and visions is another major function of prophets. Deuteronomy 13:1 lumps the prophetic and dreams together as one: "If a prophet or a dreamer of dreams arises among you...." And the familiar prophecy of Joel 2:28 concerning the coming of the Holy Spirit upon the Church in the endtimes says it in the context of dreams and visions: "And it will come about after this that I will pour out My Spirit on all mankind; and your sons and daughters will prophesy, your old men will dream dreams, your young men will see visions."

Joseph arose to power by interpreting the dreams of the Pharaoh (see Gen. 40–41), and Daniel rose to prominence interpreting King Nebuchadnezzar's dreams (see Dan. 2). Whoever desires to be the Lord's prophet today should learn to become as expert as possible in the art of understanding and responding properly to God's purposes spoken through dreams and visions. (I recommend our books and those of Bishop Bill Hamon, as well as *Dreams and Visions* by Bishop Bill's daughter-in-law, Jane Hamon.)

To remind you of what was said earlier: When God speaks through dreams and visions and other ways of dark speech, it is because He wants to do so for His purposes of enlisting us in pondering, praying, and waiting for His wisdom before acting. Prophets who reveal meanings too soon may undo God's purposes. We need to learn how to invoke others into God's processes of pondering and waiting for clarity before acting presumptuously.

### EQUIP THE SAINTS FOR MINISTRY

It is the prophet's primary purpose and task to equip the Body of Christ for ministry. In fact, Ephesians 4:11-12 lays this purpose out as a mandate for all five offices. I used to weep in my spirit before every teaching because this word had so laid hold of my heart that it grieved me to be exalted as the teaching one when I wanted each and every other to be raised up. Jeremiah 31:34 has also gripped my heart: "And they shall not teach again, each man his neighbor and each man his brother, saying, 'Know the Lord,' for they shall all know Me, from the least of them to the greatest of them...." I longed for that day when the glory locked up in each heart would be so released and manifested that teaching would no longer be necessary, and grieved that at present it remained a necessity.

Equipping others is primary to the prophetic office perhaps as much or more than to all the other five, including the office of teaching. Why? Because the gifting of the office of the prophet tends in itself to exalt and set us apart as unique and different, not so capable of emulation as the functions of the other four offices. Prophets tend to stand out whenever their works become seen. Pastors and teachers are complimented when brilliant teachings and sermons touch peoples' hearts, but hopefully it is what they have imparted that lives on more in the hearts and minds of the people rather than who they are.

Tragically, it's not so much so with prophets. People tend to—more often than with the other offices—fasten their eyes on the prophet rather than on the Lord or His teachings. Therefore I say prophets must work more assiduously to equip others and raise up others. A prophet who seeks the limelight is either immature or false. True prophets seek to be hidden and take joy in causing others to function in high gifting more than they rejoice about their own gifts.

## Work for Unity

In our time our Father is answering His Son's prayer in John 17. A basic calling upon every office and every humble Christian is to work for unity. To us this is a prerequisite. The calling upon Elijah House is to work to restore all things before our Lord's return (see Mt. 17:11), and to us nothing is more needful than the restoration of unity in the Church, among nations and in all mankind. Reconciliation between churches and denominations, ethnic groups, nations, and all the way down to the most basic units of society—brothers and sisters, children and parents, marital couples, relatives and friends, bosses and employees—is quintessential to the restoration of unity anywhere and everywhere. Prophets are gifted with insights for this very purpose, to overcome divisiveness and resultant divisions between all classes and types of people, and eventually between mankind and nature itself (see Eph. 4:1-4 about unity and Rom. 8:18 about how that may eventually affect nature).

It should go without saying that whatever prophet calls for sundering apart from others is ipso facto a false prophet! Whoever calls another branch of the Lord's Church the "whore church" is himself a whore, serving the false idol of his own supposed superiority! In actual fact, no branch of the Church and no one person has a corner on error. We are all the whore church, needing one another's corrections and ministries to be made whole and free from corruption.

Prophets, indeed all of us, must learn above all to love what and whom the Lord loves. We preach individual salvation, but the Lord preached the Kingdom of God. The Lord loves every individual and the corporateness of who and what we are as a Church and as parts of the body of mankind. Jesus' love must corral all our passions until we shudder with remorse and then repentance if ever a word or deed that would tend to create division slips past our guard.

This calling will become more and more confusing to many as the endtime climaxes. And that fact will call for more incisive words of prophetic clarification. Why confusing? Because the biblical prophetic words of the endtime warn against the coming of the one world government, and that engenders fear in the hearts of many each time the Church and the world seem to be drawing nearer to one another in oneness.

In November 1996, the first meeting of the World Christian Gathering of Indigenous Peoples (WCGIP) occurred in Rotorua, New Zealand. I rejoiced in tears of joy for the Lord as His people from many tribes and nations came together and shared their songs and dances to the glory of the Lord. A great work of unity and redemption was in progress.

During the meeting, John Dawson, one of the founders of the WCGIP, and I met together for lunch. He told me that on his desk was a tall stack of letters castigating him roundly for being part of the creation of the one-church-one-world government of the endtimes! Did he not know he was serving the devil in calling people together like that?! These benighted souls did not know the difference between what the Holy Spirit unites and what flesh draws together. They had no proper discernment, perhaps mainly because they had not learned to love what and whom Jesus loves.

As time goes on and the Holy Spirit draws His people together more and more, a demarcation line will be drawn. Those who truly know and love our Lord and have learned to love whom and what He loves will rejoice in what the Holy Spirit is doing and become an integral part of His move to create and sustain the *unity of the Spirit* until it becomes everywhere the fullness of the *unity of the faith* (Eph. 4:3,13). Regrettably, other Christians will oppose, not knowing they oppose the Lord, thinking they are opposing those who serve the devil's false unifications when the reverse will be the truth.

The call here is to those who, like John Dawson, will find themselves under attack. Be eager to maintain the unity of the Spirit by continuing to love those who persecute. Don't try to convince. Don't argue. God will eventually rescue His own from faulty paths. It is not first a mental matter; it is a matter of wounded hearts needing somewhere to fuss. Your part is simply to keep on working for reconciliation and unity. "But shun foolish controversies...about the Law; for they are unprofitable and worthless" (Titus 3:9). Just love. God will have His way in the end.

## CALL FOR INTERCESSION AND REPENTANCE

Perhaps there is no more important and defining function for New Testament prophets than the work of burden bearing and intercession, and the continual need to call God's people into repentance. When God laid the iniquity of Israel and then Judah upon Ezekiel (see Ezek. 4:4-6), it was the first time in all of history that God had laid the iniquity of an entire people on one man. Ezekiel was thus the forerunner of burden bearing. "Bear one another's burdens, and thus fulfill the law of Christ" (Gal. 6:2).

Ezekiel was called "son of man." Jesus called Himself the "Son of Man" most likely for this very reason, to demonstrate that He was stepping into the track laid down by Ezekiel. Our Father confirmed this in Isaiah 53:4-5, "Surely our griefs He Himself bore, and our sorrows He carried; yet we ourselves esteemed Him stricken, smitten of God, and afflicted. But He was pierced through for our transgressions, He was crushed for our iniquities; the chastening for our well-being fell upon Him, and by His scourging we are healed."

One of the most important functions of prophets is to act as forerunners. Prophets discover new revelations and ways to act, which open doors for all others to follow. The Old Testament prophets, following the example of the great forerunner Moses, continued to lay down the track of monotheism in a day rife with multiple gods. In a time when gods had to be placated lest they capriciously do harm, and needed to be seduced into causing fertility by sexually abominable fertility rites, the prophets revealed a holy and loving Father God who rules all and cannot be controlled by our ritualistic manipulations. This established the "track" of monotheistic belief in a good God on which the freight of revelation about Jesus would be carried. The greatest prophet of all, Jesus, laid down the track for us all—"I am the way, the truth, and the life." We walk in the Way He opened before us.

Just so, prophets today expand the revelation begun in Ezekiel. Our first calling and task is to bear burdens in intercessory prayer, not only to call the Body of Christ into that task but much more, into burden bearing intercession as a lifestyle in Christ.

*Every prophet today must come to see himself or herself as a burden-bearing intercessor, or he or she has missed the calling of God.* Faith comes by hearing and hearing by preaching, but people require ears to hear, and often do not have them. Burden-bearing intercessory prayer is the forerunning labor that goes before to open hearts and make possible true hearing. Today the long-prophesied great awakening is beginning. It is crucial that today's prophets lead forth into the work of preparing the way of the Lord, which is what burden-bearing intercession actually is. It reaches past the mind into the depths of the heart and so loves and heals that the mind is set free to hear and the heart set free to respond. Thus the will is wooed to come "just as I am, without one plea but that Jesus' blood was shed for me."

Regrettably, to date, most of the Body and most of its prophets know nothing of burden bearing and woefully little of intercession's ways. I pray and prophesy that this will change. Many are already discovering the call to intercession; but too few have yet discovered the prerequisite aspect of burden bearing. That will change.

## EXPRESS AND MODEL GOD'S LOVE IN CHRIST

In summation, every function of prophets is an expression of God's love for mankind. Every prophet is to be controlled, measured, and tested by this one requirement, that everything he or she does is an expression of the Father's love, a modeling of the nature of our Lord Jesus Christ, an incarnation of the love of God in human flesh. To whatever degree this is not true, to that degree a prophet (or any other Christian) fails his task and purpose.

## THREE LIFESTYLE PARAMETERS TO LIVE BY

Early on in our life and ministry the Holy Spirit gave three lifestyle parameters for Paula and me. He commanded us to build practices into our natures until, even as a professional basketball player does not have to think how to dribble and pass but does so habitually, these parameters would function to control us automatically in every given situation.

First, whatever Jesus would not have allowed Himself to feel, we will not feel. That did not mean we should suppress and deny feelings. We were to let anger or hurt or whatever emotion live long enough to recognize it and commit it to prayer. What it did mean was that we would not allow ourselves to dwell in any feeling Jesus would not. This meant resentments were not to be entertained; grudges were not to be held; feelings of being put upon, rejected, abused, or persecuted were not to be allowed to live any longer than it took to get them to the cross by prayer.

Along with the three parameters we were also commanded to pray about everything instantly, silently if necessary, as events happened during the day. First Thessalonians 5:17 was to be our watchword—and is so today—"Pray without ceasing." Two requisites were to be included: one, honesty. He did not want me to say to Him, "Oh thank You for my wonderful wife" whenever Paula angered me; but "Lord, I'm angry. I'd like to react hurtfully. Bring me to death on your cross and give me Your loving answer." Which brings me to the second requirement, that the cross be central in all such praying. "Lord, I can't do right. Bring me to death on your cross. Let the Holy Spirit answer through me." The self death of our Lord is so complete that when we set out to slay ourselves and let Him live in us, as us, and for us, He doesn't wipe us out and turn us into cookie-cutter copies of Himself;

He makes us to be the most we can be. The way of life is death, for "he that would lose his life will find it." The Lord commanded that we also build the habit of flash prayers into ourselves until the practice would become automatic and instant.

Second, whatever Jesus would not have thought we will not think. Again, it may be necessary at times to mull in the dark room of hurt and trouble until issues begin to surface. But what the Lord meant was clear: Do not allow yourselves to dwell in a hurtful or erroneous way of thinking that Jesus would not have. Do not embrace and give house to wrongful ways of thinking that Jesus would have avoided. We built that discipline into all our thinking. Still today, whenever we are speaking or writing, that parameter flashes like an early warning system and checks our every thought.

Third, we will not act in any way Jesus would not have acted. An automatic built-in check was placed in us before we speak, feel, think, or act in any way—would Jesus have acted this way? If we knew He wouldn't have acted in such a way, we won't either. How many pastors and others who have fallen sexually would have remained pure had this discipline been laminated into the body's actions and reactions?

How grateful we are that early on He insisted that we build these parameters into our consciences and the habit of flash prayers into our lives. *These are the primary secrets of whatever blessedness our life has been.* We cannot take credit for them; these were disciplines the Lord Himself took pains to build into us.

We found in the process that it was easier to check ourselves from feeling, thinking, and acting wrongly than it was to determine, "Whatever Jesus would have felt I will feel, whatever He would have thought I will think, and whatever He would have done I will do." We could inhibit ourselves from doing evil by prayer and the cross, but to do the positive feeling, thinking, and acting as He would was an entirely different matter! The first required willingness to die. The second, however, demanded such an intimacy with God that His Holy Spirit would have sufficient access to express His life. We could accomplish the first by willpower; "I *will* set myself to die to self in each instance." Willpower could not accomplish the second though. *Expressing His life demanded that His resurrection life be our life, and that could only happen if we were immersed often enough in His loving Presence.* From this struggle we discovered the vital necessity of devotion and worship. If we did not have enough devotional life and corporate worship, His power was not in us to manifest His life.

So the final task of prophets is both to undergird themselves in worship and to call the Body of Christ into intimacy with Him. Tommy Tenney, in The God Chasers, and Jim Goll, in Wasted on Jesus, and others in many sermons and writings have done so admirably. My counsel is to "Get with it!" Study. And get into the renewal movement, which lavishes the loving Presence of God upon His people.

It will be a great blessing to build these three parameters and the habit of flash prayers into your life, but don't stop there. Become a worshiper. Seek His loving Presence. This alone will enable you to express the life of our Lord Jesus Christ among men.

CHAPTER TEN

# Principles of Inner Healing

(Paula)

For 40 years we have been growing in the ministry of the transformation of the inner man as the Lord has given us grace and insight to meet the depths of people's needs. We have increasingly discovered that the Lord's desire and power to set people free far surpasses our ability to discern problems and our sensitivity to apply insights appropriately. In our Christian counseling the Lord has made us particularly aware of four basic laws that affect root problems in people's lives:

1. "**Honor your father and your mother**, as the Lord your God has commanded you, that your days may be prolonged, and that it may go well with you on the land which the Lord your God gives you" (Deut. 5:16, emphasis added).

2. "**Do not judge lest you be judged**. For in the way you judge, you will be judged; and by your standard of measure, it will be measured to you" (Mt. 7:1-2, emphasis added).

3. "**Do not be deceived, God is not mocked; for whatever a man sows, this he will also reap**" (Gal. 6:7, emphasis added).

4. "**Therefore you are without excuse, every man of you who passes judgment, for in that you judge another, you condemn yourself; for you who judge practice the same things**" (Rom. 2:1, emphasis added).

Whenever we have tuned into the Lord's purposes and laid the groundwork of repentance and forgiveness in the one to whom we are ministering, we have invariably experienced the healing power of the Lord flowing through the door of prayer more powerfully than we could think or ask. Counselees are empowered to choose to forgive those who wounded them. And they are enabled to recognize and repent of what they have held in their hearts. Furthermore, they are enabled to receive forgiveness for their own sinful responses.

Again and again we have been led by the Holy Spirit to pray obediently in ways that at first we did not understand. Experiencing the undeniable and lasting fruit of those prayers, we have then delved into Scripture to understand what we have seen the Lord accomplish. All of our books concerning inner healing are a result of that long-term experience and study with the Lord, grounding everything in the Word of God.

Recognizable and predictable patterns of cause and consequence have appeared so frequently that we have been tempted to develop techniques of prayer "guaranteed to work in every situation," when properly applied. In the process the Lord has made it abundantly clear that He insists on being in charge. Ministry to others must always be a *fresh meeting* in the presence and power of the Lord and by His leading, not something accomplished first or solely by knowledge or methodologies. Patterns to look for in people's lives and ways to deal with them must always be submitted to the present moving of the Holy Spirit, or we may unwittingly "use" God to manipulate the other person by techniques we have developed. Our participation in the encounter of ministry is primarily to connect the person with Jesus, and to participate with Him in lavishing upon the person His love, thus enabling the Holy Spirit to empower the person to live in the Lord's gracious lifestyle.

## WHY DO WE NEED TO MINISTER TO THE DEPTHS OF ALREADY BORN-AGAIN CHRISTIANS?

In the first seven chapters of *Transformation of the Inner Man*, we explain more completely the biblical and theological basis for the work of ministering to Christians. It is stated more succinctly in the following section:

> *For you were formerly darkness, but now you are light in the Lord; walk as children of light (for the fruit of the light consists in all goodness and righteousness and*

*truth), trying to learn what is pleasing to the Lord* (Ephesians 5:8-10).

Many Christians are trying their best to walk as children of light, but they fail to produce the fruit of that light because they are blindsided and driven from deep within by motivations and character traits of which they have been unaware. The Bible calls these "practices" (see Col. 3:9-10). Thus, these Christians too often fall into striving, disillusionment, and condemnation.

These Christians have rightly celebrated salvation as a free gift (see Eph. 2:4-5, 3:8; Rom. 6:23), but have not understood the cost of growing up in their salvation (see 1 Pet. 2:2; Eph. 3:1-19). Nor do they fully understand that they are to *work out their salvation* in fear and trembling, for God is at work *in them* (see Phil. 2:12-13). They have celebrated with Paul that "by one offering He has perfected forever those who are *being* sanctified" (Heb. 10:14 NKJ, emphasis added), without understanding sanctification as a *process* and without acknowledging with Paul, "Not that I have already obtained it, or have already become perfect, but I press on in order that I may lay hold of that for which also I was laid hold of by Christ Jesus" (Phil. 3:12). Positionally we are made perfect by Jesus' one offering, but it takes time for us to put off the old and put on the new:

> *For you have died and your life is hidden with Christ in God. When Christ, who is our life, is revealed, then you also will be revealed with Him in glory. Therefore consider the members of your earthly body as dead to immorality, impurity, passion, evil desire, and greed, which amounts to idolatry....But now you also, put them all aside: anger, wrath, malice, slander, and abusive speech from your mouth. Do not lie to one another, since you laid aside the old self with its evil practices, and have put on the new self who is **being renewed** to a true knowledge according to the image of the One who created him.... And so, as those who have been chosen of God, holy and beloved, put on a heart of compassion, kindness, humility, gentleness and patience; bearing with one another*

*and forgiving each other, whoever has a complaint against anyone; just as the Lord forgave you, so also should you. And beyond all these things put on love, which is the perfect bond of unity. And let the peace of Christ rule in your hearts, to which indeed you were called in one body; and be thankful* (Colossians 3:3-5, 8-10,12-15, emphasis added).

Many Christians tend to press on in terms of managing behavior rather than by the renewing of their minds (see Rom. 12:2) and the receiving of a new heart and spirit within (see Ps. 51; Ezek. 36:26). However, inner transformation naturally results in changed behavior, which Christians need, but many are not aware of that need. They have not in reality done away with childish things on the cross (see 1 Cor. 3:11), but have tried to control them, while still allowing them to become a part of the "treasure" in the storehouse of the heart (Lk. 6:43-45). When out of the heart comes eruptive expressions of what has been accumulating for years, they strive all the more to control their unseemly expressions, or to rebuke the devil (who had to have raw material to work with in the first place, even if he did trigger the outburst).

But in Luke 6:46-49, Jesus commanded those who follow Him to dig deep to the foundations of life—into what was trained into the character and personality of a person in the first six years of life, including the forming of attitudes, judgments, and expectations by which all succeeding experiences are interpreted. "The lamp of the body is the eye; if therefore your eye is clear, your whole body will be full of light. But if your eye is bad, your whole body will be full of darkness" (Mt. 6:22-23a). Matthew 5:29a prescribes a drastic solution for the kind of eye that causes one to stumble: "...tear it out, and throw it from you."

Jesus is able to repair the deep cracks in our foundation and to establish us securely on the Rock—Jesus Himself. But we must give Him access through prayer. It is not enough for us to pray by ourselves for ourselves. Ephesians 2:22 tells us we are *"being built together* into a dwelling of God in the Spirit" (emphasis added). First

Peter 2:5 says we "are *being built up* as a spiritual house" (emphasis added), not building ourselves. We must learn to allow others to minister to us.

John and I are so pleased today to see more and more churches developing home groups in which people can get to know one another well enough to share honestly and pray appropriately for one another for inner healing in the love of Jesus Christ. These groups are learning how to overcome the negative aspects of character development in each other, but it is an even greater blessing that such groups often provide a healthy family atmosphere in which people who have never experienced wholesome relationships in their birth families can receive what was missing and so grow into fullness in Jesus.

Apostles, prophets, evangelists, pastors, and teachers are given to the Church "*for the equipping of the saints* for the work of service, to the building up of the Body of Christ; until we all attain to the unity of the faith, and of the knowledge of the Son of God, to a mature man, to the measure of the stature which belongs to the fulness of Christ" (Eph. 4:12-13, see verse 11 also, emphasis added). Today, more and more servants in the fivefold ministry are seeing the need for inner transformation, and are teaching the Body of Christ that our gifting must never be allowed to outgrow the formation of Christlike character.

Many Christians have tried to "forget what lies behind" (see Phil. 3:13) by ignoring the past rather than by letting the Holy Spirit search the innermost parts of the heart (see Ps. 139:23-24) in order to allow Jesus to deal specifically with deeply ingrained practices and attitudes. They have attempted to put aside the old self with its practices (see Col. 3:8-10; Eph. 4:23-32) as if those were only present external conscious expressions; whereas Jesus called the Pharisees (and us) to "clean the *inside* of the cup..." (Mt. 23:26b, emphasis added), which means to deal with the subconscious motives and practices of the heart that have not yet found fullness of death and resurrection in Jesus.

Paul said to "Take care, brethren, lest there should be in any one of you an evil, unbelieving heart, in falling away from the living God" (Heb. 3:12). Inner healing and transformation are actually evangelization of the unbelieving hearts of believing Christians!

**Example 1: Children are designed by God with certain needs.** Every child who comes into the world needs to feel wanted, welcomed, and loved unconditionally. It is important for each one to be held and rocked, played with and nurtured, as well as taught and disciplined with love and fairness appropriate to his or her age. If these needs are met in children, trust is built into their hearts. They develop ability to hold their hearts open to others; to enter into healthy relationships; to be corporate with others; and to experience intimacy with God and others in the fellowship of friendship, in the blessings and stresses among relatives, in the workplace, and in marriage socially and sexually.

If a person has not received enough wholesome affectionate touch and nurture early in life, preaching and teaching will not likely be enough to effect real and lasting change. Only our own prayers—and the loving embrace of the Holy Spirit through prayer for us by other people who love and trust Jesus—can melt a hardened heart, heal wounds, fill empty places deep inside with the perfect unconditional love of God in Jesus Christ, and cast away fear (see 1 Jn. 4:18). Only death on the cross through repentance and prayer can set us free from practiced habits—coping mechanisms in this instance—in our flesh that have been built in us during our childhood (see Gal. 2:20, 5:24).

Jesus knew that our speech may be as smooth as butter while at the same time our heart is at war (see Ps. 55:21). God has always desired truth in the *innermost being* (see Ps. 51:6). For this reason John the Baptist commanded to lay the axe to the *root* of the trees (see Mt. 3:10). Luke 6:43 tells us, "There is no good tree which produces bad fruit; nor...a bad tree which produces good fruit." Hebrews 12:15 commands us, "*See to it* that no one comes short of the grace of God; that no root of bitterness springing up causes trouble, and by it many be defiled" (emphasis added).

When we become aware of a bad fruit in our lives, we ask the Holy Spirit to reveal to us the root that produced it. We have to be willing to "dig deep to our foundation" to see if that root was formed on rock or on sand as Jesus described in Luke 6:46-49:

> *And why do you call Me, 'Lord, Lord,' and do not do what I say? Everyone who comes to Me, and hears My words, and acts upon them, I will show you whom he is like: he is like a man building a house, who dug deep and laid a foundation upon the rock; and when a flood rose, the torrent burst against that house, and could not shake it, because it had been well built. But the one who has heard, and has not acted accordingly, is like a man who built a house upon the ground without any foundation; and the torrent burst against it and immediately it collapsed, and the ruin of that house was great.*

When parents are often absent or inattentive, and children are consistently left alone to cry, those children feel rejection, emotional starvation, and abandonment. If discipline is harsh and unfair—or nonexistent—children become confused and wounded. They possess no proper parameters, no structures of self-control, no center of decision inside themselves. Consequently, they do whatever seems to gain them acceptance or approval among their peers.

If they are shamed or abused physically, emotionally, or sexually, their spirit is crushed, and their identity is destroyed. They may develop a victim mentality with no sense of their own value or glory. Their response is resentment and often manifests in rebellious behavior. Inside they wonder, *What's the matter with me?* As adults, they tend to project onto others, and often onto God, what they have felt toward their parents. They expect the worst and close their hearts in anger.

*Inadequate parenting is, above all, what creates the need for inner healing in born-anew Christians.* Conversion alone did not heal because old practices sprang back to life and had to be brought to effective death through counsel and prayer, as Hebrews 12:15 says, "See to it...that no root of bitterness *springing up* causes trouble, and by it many be defiled" (emphasis added). Unfortunately, old roots slain at conversion all too often spring back to life, hence inner healing is needed after conversion.

Shortly after John and I left our 21 years of pastoral ministry to begin a counseling ministry, our living room was filled with people nearly every day waiting for appointments. Although we didn't have a phone at first, people from a large prayer group in Spokane, who knew we were available, called a friend of ours in Coeur D'Alene to schedule times for them.

One day as I was busily working in the kitchen and John was in his office ministering to one person after another, a gentleman sat waiting for quite a while for counsel and prayer. Finally, he came to me and said, "I have to talk to someone, and I can't wait any longer. Can you help me, please?" My heart went out to him, and so he followed me into the bedroom (*not a good place to counsel anyone*, but the children were downstairs playing and I had no alternative).

We placed two chairs in the middle of the room facing each other and began to talk. He let me know that he was a psychiatrist and felt he should be able to sort things out for himself, but hadn't been able to discover the root of his problem, which was very painful for him. He felt totally blocked in relationship with his wife (whom he loved), and found himself fleeing from intimacy. He knew this behavior was wounding her and had tried his best to change, but couldn't seem to overcome his negative feelings.

After we talked a while, I suggested that we pray for insight. As we prayed silently, I had a vision of a little boy standing naked, frightened, and crying at the top of a tall staircase. Behind him toward a door was another child about his age. At the bottom of the stairs was a very angry woman wagging her finger at him and calling out loudly, "You dirty little brat! What do you think you are doing? You put your clothes back on and go to your room! You're due for a spanking! I'm so ashamed of you! You're a nasty little boy! Your friend is going home, and I don't want him to come back—ever!"

The doctor began to remember the incident—exactly as I had seen it! Actually, what he had done was mere childish "show and tell," but he had been made to feel so guilty in his nudity, and so dirty and unacceptable by his mother, that those feelings had lodged deeply in his heart and had become a wall of shame between him and his wife. In his heart he had identified his wife with his mother, causing him to reject intimacy with her.

I prayed for the Lord to reach deeply into his heart where a grown man was still experiencing the emotions of a little boy who had been so wounded and shamed. Jesus lifted away the disgrace, washed away the feelings of being dirty and unacceptable, enabled him to forgive his mother, and affirmed his manhood. I prayed blessing on him and his marriage, and for the ability to separate his thoughts of his wife from his mother. I don't remember any more details, except for his excited response, "Young lady, I don't know what your training has been, or what your credentials are, but you sure do know what you're doing!" Later, he reported with glee the wonderful changes in his heart and in his relation to his wife.

That is but one example of thousands we could share. Today there are many people, Christian as well as non-Christian, whose foundations have been built on shifting sand, or who have been badly damaged along the way, and they find life to be very threatening. Jesus, the Rock, because He loves us, wants to lay new foundations of love and strength and security in our lives. He awaits our invitation, which is a basic principle of inner healing. Our loving Lord longs to be gracious to us and desires to have compassion on us (see Is. 30:18), but in His courtesy He awaits an invitation to enter the inner sanctum of our hearts with His healing grace. The Body of Christ has understood the need for altar calls, extending invitations in evangelistic crusades, exemplifying the Lord's courtesy. In His desire to save us He won't invade, but will wait to be invited. Too often though we have failed to understand that the same need for courtesy and invitation in evangelization also applies to the heart's issues *after* we have been born anew.

Therefore, as I said above, we who are practitioners of inner healing are actually evangelists to the unbelieving hearts of believers. "Take care, brethren, lest there should be in any one of you an evil, *unbelieving heart*, in falling away from the living God" (Heb. 3:12, emphasis added). In this Scripture Paul was writing to born-anew Christians. The problems of living the Christian life are not first mental; the issues of life come from the heart (see Mt. 15:18-19). Each area of inability to live righteously in Jesus is actually an area in which our heart has not yet fully believed and appropriated to itself the efficacy of the cross for death and rebirth. Inner healing is necessary because of the hidden issues of undead flesh in our hearts.

Inner healing is thus actually an extension of our conversion experience into every area of our lives. It only takes once to be born anew and assured of Heaven, but our gracious Lord wants to extend the process of rebirth and transformation into all our old nature, until in every way, day by day, we become less like our old nature and more like Him.

How is this to be accomplished? In First Thessalonians 2:7-8 Paul gives prayer ministers a good model to follow: "But we proved to be gentle among you, as a nursing mother tenderly cares for her own children. Having thus a fond affection for you, we were well-pleased to impart to you not only the gospel of God but also our own lives, because you had become very dear to us."

First Thessalonians 2:10-12 speaks to all, but especially to men: "You are witnesses, and so is God, how devoutly and uprightly and blamelessly we behaved toward you believers; just as you know how we were exhorting and encouraging and imploring each one of you as a father would his own children, so that you may walk in a manner worthy of the God who calls you into His own kingdom and glory."

## Who Needs Inner Healing?

We *all* need inner healing! We have ministered to countless thousands of people, Christian and non-Christian, who were struggling in relationships and lacked self-esteem because they were not sufficiently nurtured early in life. They were wonderfully blessed to know that because of what Jesus accomplished on the cross it is never too late to be set free from the grip of the past. They were also thrilled to experience His unconditional love presently, through prayer, as He filled the empty places deep in their hearts and assured them of their belonging in Him and of their worth. Once they received that assurance it was much easier for them to forgive those people who had failed them as they were growing up—and beyond that, to acknowledge their own sinful reactions that had become practices in their old nature, and to repent, receive forgiveness, die to their old ways on the cross, and arise as new creatures in Christ.

**Example 2: Sometimes little children make inner vows.** Inner vows are determinations we make as little children, setting ourselves to act or not act in given ways. Vows made later in life are not as powerful because they are not conceived during formative years. Inner vows remain hidden in our hearts even into adulthood. It's like setting a computer. Years later someone presses a button, and out comes the program: "I'll never be like my parents!"; "I'll never treat my kids the way I was treated!"; "I'm never going to grow up!"; "I'll never open my heart again!"; "I'll never trust anyone again with my feelings!"

Inner vows made in formative years lock us into behavioral patterns in adulthood even though we may have forgotten making them. They program us subliminally. Our minds are much akin to computers; once a program in our mind has been set, it continues by the law of inertia to operate consistently the same way, from deep below the levels of conscious awareness and desire.

Forgotten vows are difficult to identify. All vows do not disappear during the maturation process, or even when we receive Jesus and die to self—on the contrary they resist dying on the cross. They may be expressed, for instance, as habitual defensiveness, hidden bitter expectations, automatic angers, or anxieties and fears.

When we make a condemning judgment upon another person, vowing never to do what they have done, we find that the vow sometimes works in reverse according to Matthew 7:1-3 and Romans 2:1—judging others causes us to do the very same or similar things. "I'll never discipline like my Father did"—and then find ourselves doing the very same thing with our own children, for example.

Even desirable inner vows can be harmful, since they prompt us into fleshly righteousness. For example, we may lock ourselves into being gentle in situations in which the Lord is calling us to be stern. We knew a man who had vowed never to be anything but patient, kind, and gentle—and he was unfailingly that way with his wife, which would seem to be a good thing. However, he married a very controlling and critical woman who actually needed him to stop her tirades and haul her to account. But he couldn't. Like Ahab with Jezebel, he allowed her to continue in her sinful ways. His mercy and gentleness were unsanctified. Their children were continually wounded, many of their friends became alienated, and their marriage finally ended in divorce. His wife chose to live the rest of her life in denial. All of which would have been unnecessary had he brought to death his unsanctified merciful nature on the cross and arisen to say firmly and with authority, "Stop that!" Later on he and three of their children accepted ministry of inner healing, broke free from that seemingly good inner vow, and grew beautifully in the love of the Lord from that point on.

*Godly authority in prayer, as well as repentance and forgiveness, is required to break the power of inner vows.*

**Example 3: Children who suffer repeated wounding develop bitter expectations about the way life will go.** "Here it comes again!" "This always happens to me!" When children are wounded or disappointed again and again, a cloud forms over their life. Because so many hurtful things have happened and/or promises have been broken, they can't trust, and tend to expect the worst to happen. Consequently, the power of their expectation, a message sent even silently from the heart, tends to draw the worst from people.

"Nobody likes me. I don't even like myself. You won't like me or choose me." They see the negative where it isn't, fail to hear affirmation when it is given, and often misinterpret what people say and do. If it rains on the day they plan a picnic, they're likely to take it personally.

Such bitter roots are not merely psychological expectations. They may also be, and most often are, activations of the law of sowing and reaping (see Gal. 6:7) quoted previously. Whatever we do sets in motion forces that must be reaped, either from good seeds sown, or bad. Our actions and attitudes (emotional judgments) made in childhood may not be reaped until adulthood, usually then through our spouse, boss, friends, or relatives. Repeated patterns of fruit reveal bitter root judgments made in childhood, thus we also need inner healing, to be set free from deleterious reaping, by the efficacy of the cross, applied through prayer. In addition, we need those people who can minister to us as prayer counselors because we can seldom find the objectivity to see our own fruits and roots accurately. There are no private saints, only corporate humble people willing to be seen and ministered to by others.

Bitter root judgments and expectancies are two of the most powerful forces that wreak havoc in Christian lives. Those Christians who want to maintain that judgments and expectancies died on the cross when they received Jesus find themselves tormented by continuous reaping of bad fruits. Since they cannot believe anything in them has not died on the cross, denial then gives satan a playing field to exacerbate normal reaping into crescendos of harm.

**Example 4: Are you tense, lonely, and tired? Trying too hard?** All of us develop some measure of performance orientation, because none of us were raised by perfect parents, and none of us have made sinless responses even to the good things that happened in our lives, much less the bad. Performance orientation occurs whenever little children receive and build into their nature a lie: "I'm not loved because I exist, but only if I do enough to earn it." "I don't belong because I was born into a family; I can only belong if I do right." This creates unending striving, based on fear of rejection, of not measuring up, of not being acceptable no matter how well I perform. Cultures around the world, each in their own way, relentlessly encourage the growth of performance orientation. Therefore, we all want to look good, to be noticed, appreciated, and rewarded in some way because these things tell us we are loved, whereas if we were healed of performance orientation, we would know throughout our being that God loves us anyway, just as we are, without our having to perform.

What's wrong with wanting to perform well and being reward-ed for it? We should always try to do our best; performance orienta-tion, however, has to do with wrong motives for performing. Many Christians do the right thing for the wrong reasons: "If I do the right thing, I'll belong." "If I do well enough, I'll be loved." The irony is that we are already loved and accepted; we just can't believe it. Per-formance orientation is actually at its root an inability to believe Jesus loves us unconditionally. It is precisely the unbelieving heart of Hebrews 3:12. Thus, we're never satisfied, even with tremendous success, because reaching a goal doesn't make us feel any more loved. And if we give up and quit, we really feel unlovable because of failure. Christians free of performance orientation serve the Lord simply because they love Him, but performance-oriented Christians serve from a base of fear. They *have* to serve lest they lose their place and worth in Him.

Unfortunately, there are many churches in which exhortations to do more, to do better, and to give more (or shame on you!) are preached with powerful and sometimes manipulative pressures. Sadly, many of those churches also often lack understanding of the motives of people's hearts and present little or no opportunity for the inner healing that would touch their people at deep levels and en-courage and set them free not to perform, but to serve purely out of gratitude to God for His love.

God loves us unconditionally, just as we are (but too much to leave us that way)! "God demonstrates His own love toward us, in that while we were still sinners, Christ died for us" (Rom. 5:8 NKJ). We know this Scripture mentally, but only if we receive enough inner healing to set us free from performance orientation does it become more than shibboleth words all Christians know and say but few know at heart level and can live.

**Example 5: A Heart of stone—"Nobody can hurt me now."**
When we have experienced various kinds of wounding, we tend to
withdraw, hide, harden our hearts, and build self-protective walls
about ourselves. Behind our walls we keep the ammunition of memories of unforgiven injustices to hurl at anyone who seems to threat-
en. We harden our hearts and think to isolate ourselves from those
who might hurt us. But a wall is a wall. It keeps out the good as well
as the bad. Hearts of stone prevent true fellowship. We go through
the motions, but our heart is not in it, either with God or our fellow
human beings.

Thankfully we don't have to stay behind that wall. The Bible
offers us a promise: "I will give you a new heart and put a new [per-
sonal] spirit within you; I will take the heart of stone out of your
flesh [your sinful flesh], and give you a heart of flesh [kind, loving,
compassionate, sensitive]. I will put My Spirit [the Holy Spirit]
within you and cause you to walk in My statutes, and you will keep
My judgments and do them" (Ezek. 36:26-27 NKJ).

We teach people to invite others to pray for God to melt their
hardness of heart, to pour in His love, to fill their hungry places with
His nurture, and to heal their wounds with His holy medicine, and
also to pray for strength of spirit to choose to forgive and hold their
hearts open.

**Example 6: God, is that really You?** When we have not allowed the Lord to accomplish healing in our innermost being, we
tend to see everything, even God, "in a mirror dimly" (see 1 Cor.
13:12). We continue to look through the colored glasses of our childhood wounds. We can't see clearly because our childish perceptions
are projected onto today's experiences and onto God.

When requesting inner healing, we pray for the inner child to
be healed and comforted. We pray that habitual childish ways of
thinking, feeling, and acting will be put to death on the cross along
with whatever projected images and pictures have been revealed in
our memory stream as actively blinding and binding.

We teach people to confess and repent of sinful responses to
hurts—to choose to forgive and receive healing for wounds, and

forgiveness for responses—to receive a new heart, a new spirit, a re-newed mind, and strength to walk in the new way (see Rom. 6:4b), until people can take hold of what Jesus has already accomplished on the cross and until they come into the fullness of their inheritance (see Phil. 3:8-15; Eph. 3:16-19).

*We can't wear God's armor **and** our own protective clothing.* As we choose forgiveness and begin walking in the new way, we can learn to "put on the whole armor of God, that [we] may be able to stand against the wiles of the devil" (Eph. 6:11 NKJ).

## GOD NEVER LEAVES US; HE ALWAYS LOVES US

Transformation is a process, not an event! The Holy Spirit will reveal to us, over time, the things that still lie hidden in our hearts.

*I am conscious of nothing against myself, yet I am not by this acquitted; but the one who examines me is the Lord. Therefore do not go on passing judgment before the time, but wait until the Lord comes who will both bring to light the things hidden in the darkness and disclose the mo-tives of men's hearts; and then each man's praise will come to him from God* (1 Corinthians 4:4-5).

Jesus accomplished death of our sinful natures on the cross so we would have the power to walk in the new way, no longer slaves to our old habits of thinking, feeling, and behaving. Romans 6:6 says, "Knowing this, that our old self was crucified with Him, that our body of sin might be done away with, that we should no longer be slaves to sin." Jesus wrought this accomplishment, but we must choose to take hold of it.

*Transformation is a process, not an event* (Phil. 3:12b)! It re-quires discipline to walk in the new way. When an old habit threat-ens, we must present it to the Lord immediately, honestly confessing, and asking for His power to help us turn the other way, "taking every thought captive to the obedience of Christ" (2 Cor. 10:5b). "Even so consider yourselves to be dead to sin, but alive to God in Christ Jesus" (Rom. 6:11). "I have been crucified with Christ; and it is no longer I who live, but Christ lives in me; and the life which I now live in the flesh I live by faith in the Son of God, who loved me, and delivered Himself up for me" (Gal. 2:20, emphasis added).

*This process is not striving, but discipline.* Romans 6:12-13 says, "Therefore do not let sin reign in your mortal body that you should obey its lusts, and do not go on presenting the members of your body to sin as instruments of unrighteousness; but present yourselves to God as those alive from the dead, and your members as instruments of righteousness to God."

*Notice, this is **our** part.* "Now those who belong to Christ Jesus have crucified the flesh with its passions and desires" (Gal. 5:24).

Ephesians 6:18 says, "Pray at all times in the Spirit." When we do this, we are agreeing with God, allowing *Him*—not sin—to reign in us. "For sin shall not be master over you, for you are not under law, but under grace" (Rom. 6:14).

## CALLED TO MINISTER DEEPER THAN HEALING OF MEMORIES
### (JOHN ADDS TO THE STORY)

We had pioneered in inner healing for several years when there came a day in which the Lord said, "You'll not be working in the healing of memories in the coming days." That startled us. We thought, *Is He calling us out of inner healing?* But He kept sending people for healing, so we knew that wasn't what He meant. Then He began to send us people whose problems lay deeper in origin than in anyone who had come before. The Holy Spirit revealed levels of re-action and sinful responses way below conscious recollection of memories. We were dealing with subliminal issues beyond people's ability to recall specific memories. These issues had to be discovered by more careful questioning and by gifts of knowledge in the Holy Spirit.

We began to deal with problems in people that had arisen in their birth experience, at nursing time, and in their first two years— long before people could consciously recall what their spirit re-membered and reacted to. And then He led us beyond that into prenatal experiences and how they affect character development. Truly, though in many people we were still dealing with conscious memories, in other people we had moved far beneath and beyond the healing of memories, as He had said we would.

For example, to speak of our own stories rather than expose others, I had always been an athlete, not at all bothered by pain as I would crash against the walls in racquetball, for instance. But if a nurse came toward me with a needle, I fought to control feelings of panic. It didn't make sense. I had also wondered why I didn't trust doctors. My mother and then Paula had to scold to get me to take prescribed medicines. It also puzzled me why I reacted strongly when anyone seemed to be hurrying me. "I'll get there in my own time, thank you!" And I was often late even when there was no reason causing me to be tardy.

Then the Lord opened the field of prenatal and birth experiences to us—and things began to make sense. When my mother went into labor, her doctor shot her with a long needle, three times, trying to make her deliver faster because he wanted to go to a party. My parents learned later that the medicine he used could and should have killed both her and me. She was a very strong girl who had ridden a horse to school five miles and back every day. It had required three nurses to hold her muscles back when she had had an appendectomy, and just tussling with my father in fun she had broken two of his ribs when she fisted him in the chest. With those powerful muscles she fairly shot me like a cannon ball into the world!

By the time we learned these facts about my birth, the Lord had made us aware that we have a mind in our spirit that knows, discerns, and reacts even before the brain and conscious mind are formed and active—even as John the Baptist, six months along in his mother's womb, leaped for joy when Mary entered the room carrying our Lord Jesus (see Lk. 1:44). When people prayed for my healing, I knew in my spirit that I had known then that the medicine the doctor used could have killed me. I "knew" I had been forced to expend energy to stay alive. It was easy then to see why I didn't trust doctors or medicines, feared needles, and refused to be hurried. I have now been so healed that I trust doctors easily, have no difficulty taking medicines, no longer react when people try to hurry me, and am seldom tardy.

When Paula and I first began to teach together, each for five minutes or so, back and forth, Paula was extremely reluctant to venture out to express what she thought on her own. She wore me out, continually checking to see what I thought she ought to say, or thought she should have said. I kept saying, "Take your liberty. You know the material. I'll trust you to say it rightly." But she would hang back. She had always been extremely shy. In the beginning I had to practically force her to answer a telephone.

And other things about her puzzled us. For instance, Paula floats like a cork. She is so buoyant she can't even get below the water to swim underwater. But she was afraid to let her face go below the surface, swimming awkwardly with her head held way above the water line. If a blanket slipped over her head in the night, or if I kissed her too long, she had a moment of panic.

Then the Lord revealed how to understand prenatal reactions and heal them. Before Paula was born, her mother had suffered a burst appendix and peritonitis had set in. Before there were miracle drugs and before doctors knew how to make little buttonhole incisions for appendectomies, they had slit her open from side to side, and used drains to carry away infectious matter. She nearly died. She slowly recovered, but the doctors warned her not to get pregnant too soon because her swelling abdomen might cause the stitches to burst open. But she became almost immediately pregnant with Paula. Her physician wrapped her with tight binders, which she wore all during the pregnancy.

When Paula's mother came to visit once and happened to share with Paula that history, revelation leaped to our minds. Paula had been terribly afraid in the water of the womb, imbibing her mother's fear through burden bearing, and feeling her own fear of being miscarried. Of course she was afraid to be submerged in water! Paula knew in the womb that as she grew in size, she was endangering both her mother and herself. Likewise, she was afraid to grow in spiritual size in our new venture of growing together—somehow subliminally she was afraid that if she allowed herself to grow in the Lord, that would endanger me, and her.

Also, her mother had been ambivalent while carrying her. She wanted her baby, but on the other hand was fearful and did not want to be pregnant. Paula was aware of those feelings intuitively in the womb, and so cried all the time when she was born, and could be consoled only by her father, who very much wanted her. When friends prayed for Paula for prenatal healing, all her symptoms disappeared and Paula was free. She even beats me to the phone, and I'm the one who resists answering "devil telephone."

Since those first days of discovery, we have prayed for thousands of people about hundreds of issues and reactions below the level of conscious memory. How do we know what is there? First, by tracking from fruits to roots. We and our staff have now such a backlog of experience that we can tell when most likely there have been prenatal, birth, or infant traumas. How can we confirm our hunches and find out the facts? 1.) from symptoms and events in the present, 2.) by asking about personal and family history, (a) what parents and others have told the client about his or her early life, and (b) by interviewing relatives whenever possible; 3.) by asking the Holy Spirit to reveal by gifts of knowledge.

It has been amazing how clearly the Lord can reveal to us what needs to be seen and prayed about, though we have learned not to lay heavy revelations on people and say God said this or that. We may say, "Here's what I think the Lord is showing me....Could you check it out with family members?" Or, when family members have passed on or can't be consulted, "Think on this possibility. How does it witness to you?" We are careful not to create false memories by suggestion.

### CAN THIS AREA OF REVELATION BE JUSTIFIED THEOLOGICALLY AND SCRIPTURALLY? (PAULA SPEAKS)

To born-again Christians it was said:

*And do not participate in the unfruitful deeds of darkness, but instead even expose them; for it is disgraceful*

*even to speak of the things which are done by them in se-*
*cret. But **all things become visible when they are ex-***
***posed by the light, for everything that becomes visible is***
***light**. For this reason it says, "Awake, sleeper, and arise*
*from the dead, and Christ will shine on you"* (Ephesians
5:11-14, emphasis added).

We, the Body of Christ, the Church, have been that sleeper.
Though our old self has been crucified with Him, it refuses to stay
dead. Therefore we have attempted to "die daily" (see 1 Cor. 15:31),
but often we try to do so by willful efforts to conform to Christian
standards exteriorly rather than digging down to the deep roots of
our formation as our Lord commanded. We understand that John the
Baptist said to "lay the axe to the root of the trees," but we have not
yet fully comprehended how roots lie hidden, beneath the surface,
and that the very first events of our life—en utero and at birth—
comprise the deepest roots. Therefore we have not yet experienced
the breadth of that process of inner sanctification and laying down
our life by which we can come into the fullness of resurrection life
and power. Our Lord is concerned with the transformation of the unbelieving heart of believers—at the deepest levels (see Heb. 3:12).

Our book, *Healing the Wounded Spirit*, deals with those deep
wounds and sins of our personal spirit, and is another step inward to
the deep revelation and the inner transformation that leads to living
in the fullness of our inheritance in the Lord. We offer to our readers what the Lord has given to us, for no one after lighting a lamp
hides it in a container, or puts it under a bed; but he puts it on a lamp
stand, in order that those who come in may see the light. For nothing
is hidden that shall not become evident, nor anything secret that shall
not be known and come to light (see Lk. 8:16-17).

John and I have risked being vulnerable as we have shared certain insights (concerning our personal spirit from the time of conception) that seem to some people not to be so clearly laid out in the
Word of God as were our earlier teachings. However, we direct those
people who are interested in studying the Word of God about these

matters to the following Scriptures: Psalm 58:3, Isaiah 48:8, Psalm 51:5-6 (NIV), Job 32:8, Luke 1:38,41-44.

In these areas, as John said, we have often depended first on the Holy Spirit's gifts of knowledge and perception for discovery, and the tests of time and effectiveness for validation. Literally hundreds of thousands have received deep healing through prayer for prenatal wounds and birth trauma (by us and the many who have learned from us). Further validation has come in recent years from tremendous amounts of scientific research, notably as reported by Dr. Thomas Verny, in his book, *The Secret Life of the Unborn Child.*

Many times we have had to take an "Emmaus walk" with the Lord for Him to reveal to us what was always in the Scriptures but hidden to our understanding. We expect to continue to do so. We invite our readers to do the same with all that seems unfamiliar and perhaps threatening. Ponder new concepts in the heart, lift them to Him, and "take care how you listen; for whoever has, to him shall more be given; and whoever does not have, even what he thinks he has shall be taken away from him" (Lk. 8:18).

"To him who has shall more be given." Has what? We believe this to mean trust—ability to risk venturing beyond the confines of what we thought we knew into that which God would reveal for the healing of others. Many people bury the talents of revelation God would have given because they can't trust Him enough to risk error. Those who can trust, know God is able to restore and make good of all things, even our mistakes (see Rom. 8:28). Those who can trust, grow into the "love of Christ which *surpasses knowledge*" (Eph. 3:19a, emphasis added). Like Paul, we are "confident of this very thing, that He who began a good work in you will perfect it until the day of Christ Jesus" (Phil. 1:6).

What now seems strange, risky, and new will eventually be familiar, safe ground because forerunner pilgrims will have tracked out safe paths to walk in. Blessed are those whose trusting hearts enable them to venture early upon the high seas of revelation that set many free. The first people who are declared unfit for the Kingdom of God (in Revelation 21:8) are the "cowardly and unbelieving," then come the abominable and murderers and immoral persons and so on. Our hope is that more and more Christians will be willing like Peter to step out of the boat onto the stormy seas of faith.

CHAPTER ELEVEN

# TESTIMONIES, ENDORSEMENTS, AND KEYS

(PAULA)

John and I have found it embarrassing to include in this book, or anywhere, effusive testimonies about ourselves and our ministry, but are doing so because testimonies seem the best way to reveal the worldwide scope and depth of transformation and healing that our Lord has accomplished over the years. We hope these give you some idea of what inner healing is and how far it has reached.

**Card from a teenage girl in Germany:** "You gave me once more, more than a glimpse of light. I want to thank you; thank the Lord our God for your visit, for your teaching, for your love. Thank you for your serving, the unconditional loving way you do. Thank you for being so much 'Sonshine.' Thank you for reflecting His love. We need parents, models, people like you so much. You give hope and courage to walk through the desert. You are two of those 'position lights' that show us new orientation in this fog of the end time. No, you are *one light* as man and woman together. It's like balm seeing a couple like you. I love you—and you are real—God is real—*living, alive*—and I just had another 'confirmation' by meeting you. May God continue blessing you and the seeds. Let me hug you very very much. See you again one day and in the meantime I share the presence of the Lord by studying the Bible and your books."

**From Resurrection Christian Ministries, St. Louis, Missouri:** "The two schools we sponsored for you at Palatine Convent were memorable: a packed house of residents from all over the country—including Christian psychologists who still think it was the best seminar they ever attended! We love you, we bless you, we pray for your continued spiritual growth and anointing."

Paula's comment: This group of psychiatrists wanted to know how they could bring Christianity into their practice. We were stunned that they didn't already know! We found that they had separated the physical from the spiritual in their minds, compartmentalizing so that they had no awareness that the Holy Spirit in them was active with their own spirit in every session with every person. They did not realize that they were already spiritual in everything they do. They may have been seeking a program to follow to make it so. We explained to them that the sincerity of their devotion to Jesus Christ and the reality of His living in and expressing through them day by day already brings Christianity into their practice, and that since the Holy Spirit lives in them, the Lord has opportunity to draw people to Himself. They responded with quiet but joyful amazement.

**From a couple who worked with Elijah House, and remain friends:** "What a blessing it was to be a part of Elijah House, both in house and on the field. When we saw how effective this ministry is, no matter what country, what language, we realized that we were really seeing eternal truths being applied. God's hand was in all of this! Elijah House is not a destination—it is a way-station. This is a place of being transformed and equipped to carry on. The ministry isn't limited to a geographical location, or even to designated 'leaders.' We have shared the privilege and experience of ministry in Australia and Finland, as well as at home. We were not only *changed* by the ministry; we were also equipped to share the ministry. Perhaps that is the greatest gift of all—sharing the heart of God with hurting hearts."

**From Transformation Ministry in Newtown, Connecticut:** "Thank you for paving the way for us and so many others. Thank you, John and Paula, for your personal ministry and friendship. Many meaningful memories, especially your marrying us on March 27, 1986, on the Mount of Transfiguration in Israel with Paula as Shelvy's Matron of Honor. We are humbled and blessed to be an Elijah couple—carrying on the vision in the Northeast."

**From Elijah House in Austria:** "It says in Psalm 1, 'Blessed is the man [ministry] whose delight is in the law of the Lord....It is like a tree planted by streams of water; it yields its fruit in season. Whatever it does prospers.' Of course we don't consider your location by the Spokane river to be the reason for your fruitfulness, but the River of Life, He Himself washing through you, purifying, nourishing and bringing the fruitfulness of your work (Jn. 15:16). Thanks for all you have given us, through friendship, example, and for all the wisdom you taught us during our training. We are now grateful to be producing much fruit here in this part of the world."

**From the former coleader of Elijah House East (Washington D.C. area):** "Elijah House East was greatly affected by your ministry and the wealth of revelation given for God's glory and the healing of the Body of Christ. We touched deeply thousands of lives in our counseling and teaching and in turn many of them have touched many others deeply. I could write several books of testimonies of healed lives and restored families who have new generational paths to walk and who, themselves, have come to be called the 'repairers of the breach.' "

Paula's comment: Lewelly N. Fletcher, her husband and coleader, whom we simply called "Fletch," has been restored to his Father and is waiting within that great cloud of witnesses, and I believe, cheering us on and interceding for us. We have had numerous reports of the powerful effect Elijah House East has had on our East Coast and Canada. We are happy to have Betty Fletcher working with us now at our home base in Idaho.

### ASSORTED MESSAGES IN THE MAIL:

"I read Isaiah 32 as my daily devotion. Verse 2 really caught my attention. 'Each man will be like a shelter from the wind and a refuge from the storm, like streams of water in the desert, and the shadow of a great rock in a thirsty land.' Isaiah 32 certainly describes what John and Paula's ministry has been to so very many people. Within the context of Isaiah 32, this verse also describes perhaps the most important impact Elijah House has had on the Body of Christ— raising 'each man' to minister to the Body of Christ."

"You guys are a blessing and we're thankful for everything that we have learned from you personally and from your books. We've never gotten along better than we are now, and have never before sensed more of an appreciation for each other. We both believe that our marriage was saved because of the very few days we were able to spend with you guys back in 1996. We cannot imagine where we would be today if God had not orchestrated those events."

"Thanks a lot for seeking the Lord and learning from Him, and passing on these tools to us. I rejoice over all the new insight—and I can't wait to pass it on to everybody who wants to hear, and to minister and see people being set free. God bless you!"

"My generation is so hungry for elders in the church to direct and guide them, and I just thank you that you have not resigned yourselves to the sidelines in retirement like so many others. Thank you for filling some of that hunger in me this weekend. In Christ."

"Thanking Father God for you and all I am gleaning from these tapes. What a gold mine of wisdom, understanding, and experience you have—insights into human nature. I loved it when you said you were 'Garbage Collectors!' You are so funny, real, human, compatible, and make each other shine so beautifully. Thank God you can touch God's heart in prayer on behalf of so many—and take to Him the root causes of our problems—so God can set us free! Keep hauling the trash out, and help the Bride to make herself ready for the Bridegroom! Praying the Lord's favor and blessings continue to flow on you and your dear family. You are a unique gift to the Body. With lots of love and gratefulness."

"Thanks for a really solid piece of teaching illustrated by the integrity of your lives."

## The Healed and Transformed Life of Ivanka May

"Mine is a story of wounding from the beginning of my life. I am one of those many lives John and Paula touched through their passion to reach hearts for Jesus. My parents were Yugoslavian. I was born in Europe during the Second World War. My father especially did not want the responsibility of caring for a baby in such a dangerous and war-torn time and place. At his urging my mother went to a doctor and tried unsuccessfully three times by chemical injection to have me aborted.

"My mother was very lonely and afraid as she remained with me in Vienna while my father, a journalist, had to spend a great deal of time in Berlin. As a very little child I didn't know the presence and comfort of a father. Anxiety turned to terror when our family experienced the Dresden fire bombing. However, we were among the very few to survive.

"For a little while we stayed with a German family I learned to love, and then we had to leave the country. We emigrated to Argentina. This was a painful beginning again for my family. We had lost everything—land, a beautiful home, friends, and valuable possessions. My father felt the loss especially because as a successful educated man he had been able to feel good about himself and share with others. Now he had no dignity, nor any way to provide adequately for his family. Our home in Argentina began with a dirt floor.

"Life for me had been a series of physical and emotional traumas. Then, when I entered school, I found it was difficult. For one thing, this was the third language I was expected to learn. Though I was not fully aware of it, I had developed a serious hormonal problem that prevented my coming into puberty. In my teens, I became aware that there was something wrong when I recognized that I had not developed physically as other young women had.

"When I moved to be with my aunt in the United States, I was fortunate to meet a wonderful group of Christians. My mother had told me about God, and we sometimes prayed, but one of my new friends in America led me to the Lord Jesus. The group became a supportive and encouraging fellowship for me to meet with. We enabled each other to grow individually and as a family in Christ. The lady who led me to the Lord gave me many of John and Paula Sandford's tapes to listen to, and they ministered to me, keeping me under their wings of intercession.

"I met the Sandfords at Tolentine Center in Chicago in the spring of 1978. I came with a group of friends and heard teachings about inner healing. At that time Paula and John ministered to me concerning the attempted abortion. They took my parents' place and asked my forgiveness. They also prayed, breaking an inner vow I had made not to grow up. Later John came and spoke at my church on the subject of spiritual rebellion. He told me to pray daily, "I choose life." I did that for three years!

"Any time the Sandfords came anywhere close, I went to hear them teach. As I grew, they remarked about the new life they saw in me. I was actually enjoying life! My group as well as the Sandfords continued to pray for me.

"The kind of transformation that this ministry brings is usually a process, as it was with me. But I must say the changes in me were quite significant, to the point that people saw them. The "life" awakening that came to my spirit as well as to my body was certainly noticeable! I will never forget my doctor's pointing out the changes in my body, and I was then in my early thirties. [She actually developed a full bosom at 35!]

"Many blessings followed—a new relationship with my father. He and my mother eventually moved and settled near me. As I received new life I started sharing with others. My husband and I had the privilege of caring for my mother in her older years.

"I am immensely grateful for John and Paula for what God has done through them. I am grateful for the fullness of life I experience! Thank you, Lord, for there is always a way! And thank you, Lord, that I, Ivanka May, have opportunity through Elijah House to bring life to many others!"

Paula's comment: Ivanka is now one of our Elijah House counselor/ teachers, and a very dear friend and spiritual daughter, whom we love and are proud of.

### BIBLICAL COUNSELING: INNER HEALING AND TRANSFORMATION, A KEY TO FULFILLING GOD'S PURPOSES

As important as inner healing is for sanctification and transformation of individual lives, God's purposes are of greater magnitude. Inner healing and transformation are vital keys to the success of many things that are God's calling and emphases in the Body of Christ today.

## 1. Renewal

God's sovereign outpouring of love in the renewal that began January 20, 1994, in Toronto, Canada, goes hand in hand with inner healing. The more of God's love we experience, the more we are capable of dealing with the hurtful and negative things still lodged in our hearts. The more we allow the things lodged in our hearts to be taken to the cross through repentance and forgiveness, the more we are able to experience God's love. Are we willing to soak in God's presence and receive? Will we allow love to melt our hearts? Can we let go of the familiar and risk looking foolish? Are we afraid of persecution? Does our need to control sometimes quench the Holy Spirit?

It is the belief of many in the renewal movement that without inner healing and transformation, the renewal movement will not last. Along with the renewal that we've witnessed in Toronto, we've also seen more and more people healed innerly, and more in love with Jesus. Few people come to Toronto, or to renewal anywhere, seeking manifestations. Most come to receive more of Jesus' love and healing, and to be trained to serve Him in outreaches all over the world. Renewal has been going on for more than 17 years in Argentina, and we are informed that 90 percent of their converts continue to grow because they are very soon ministered to with inner healing and deliverance, and are taught to help others. The Bible says we are known by our fruit.

## 2. Spiritual Warfare

Without inner healing and transformation, we may be running onto battlefields with great gaping holes in our armor—carrying a lot of baggage from our childhood, unhealed wounds or sinful self-protections, anger, unforgiveness, etc. As Christians we should be hidden in Christ, but in warfare we are exposed. Do we have wisdom to pray hiding prayers? Do we trust and honor authority? Can we humble ourselves to receive help, or are we prideful? Can we be part of a team, listen to others, follow directions, and accept ministry? Do we value being tested and disciplined? Lone rangers make easy targets. Do we wait on the Lord; are we secure in Him? Are we being transformed in character so that we are secure from our own deficits on the battlefields of warfare?

### 3. Intercession

Intercession begins in the heart of God. Intercession is not begging or manipulating to cause God to do something He doesn't want to do, or is reluctant to do. We learn to respond to *His* call, and invite Him to do what *He* has already purposed to do. We must develop an intimate relationship with Him to be able to grow in ability to hear His voice—in order to determine what *He* calls us to pray about.

Without sufficient cleansing and healing of our hearts through inner healing, we may see and hear inaccurately, with unhealed eyes and ears. We may then tend to project our own problems and agendas— our need to fix something—onto people and situations not yet ripe. The trouble we see may be real, but it is would not be wise to pour water on a fire God is building, for instance, or in another case, light a fire to try to make God move. Without enough inner healing for transformation of character, our intercessions will be marked by errors and projections of our own problems.

### 4. Deliverance

We may be delivered from a demonic influence without inner healing. However without that healing that brings repentance and forgiveness and puts to death on the cross the character structures within us that serve as houses for the demonic, a demon may return later with seven worse than himself, as Jesus Himself warned in Luke 11:24-26:

> *When the unclean spirit goes out of a man, it passes through waterless places seeking rest, and not finding any, it says, "I will return to my house from which I came." And when it comes, it finds it swept and put in order. Then it goes and takes along seven other spirits more evil than itself, and they go in and live there; and the last state of that man becomes worse than the first.*

Deliverance and inner healing go hand in hand, which is the central theme and teaching of our book, *A Comprehensive Guide to*

*Deliverance and Inner Healing.* Deliverance without confession, repentance, and forgiveness is dangerous. In many cases, inner healing without deliverance may be ineffective.

## 5. Unity

Jesus' passionate prayer in John 17 was for unity. Psalm 133 declares unity between brothers to be the relationship upon which God commands His blessing—life forevermore. Ephesians 2:20-22 speaks of the whole building of the Church being fitted together, growing into a holy temple in the Lord, built together into a dwelling place of God in the Spirit. Ephesians 4:3 calls us to be diligent to preserve the unity of the Spirit in the bond of peace. Ephesians 4:12-13 speaks of equipping the saints for the work of service to the building up of the Body of Christ until we all attain to unity of faith.

We are supposed to speak the truth in love, to grow up into Christ, whom the whole Body, according to the proper working of each individual part, causes growth of the Body for the building up of itself in love. But if we remain unhealed innerly, what we speak and do may not effect unity at all, rather division and hurt. When we discover parts in us that are sick—in ourselves or in others who disturb the peace—we shouldn't amputate; instead we need to heal and transform from weaknesses to strengths, from degradations to glory, as in Isaiah 51:3: "Indeed, the Lord will comfort Zion; He will comfort all her waste places. And her wilderness He will make like Eden, and her desert like the garden of the Lord; joy and gladness will be found in her, thanksgiving and sound of a melody."

Only if our hearts are sufficiently transformed can we maintain the gracious lifestyle that prevents animosities and sustains unity. Ephesians 4:23-24 says we are to lay aside the old self, put on the new self in God's likeness, and be renewed in the spirit of our mind—which is what the ministry of inner healing and transformation is all about.

## 6. Evangelism

Jesus prayed passionately that we be perfected in unity so that the world would know that God sent Him. *We* are the message more powerfully than our words can say. We must be healed and transformed more and more into *His* image in order to represent Him well.

Thousands of people are being converted today, and are asking, "Now what?" Many are hanging onto their old ways and beliefs as well as their faith in Christ, just to cover all the bases. We must disciple them, bringing healing and transformation to them so they can *grow up* in their salvation! Hebrews 3:12 says, "Take care, brethren, lest there should be in any one of you *an evil, unbelieving heart*, in falling away from the living God" (emphasis added).

Areas in our lives in which we cannot manifest the nature of our Lord are actually regions inside our hearts that have not yet allowed the grace of God in Christ to bring those parts to effective death and rebirth, and thus to transformation into His likeness. The call upon us is not only to bring the gospel to the world so that all may be converted, but to also evangelize the unbelieving hearts of believers!

### 7. Reconciliation

Within families, among friends, between churches and tribes and nations, reconciliation necessitates repentance and forgiveness, the very essence of inner healing and transformation.

Second Corinthians 5:19-20 says: "God was in Christ reconciling the world to Himself, not counting their trespasses against them, and He has committed to us the word of reconciliation. Therefore, we are ambassadors for Christ, as though God were entreating through us; we beg you on behalf of Christ, be reconciled to God." **This is our call in Elijah House** as we attempt to fulfill Matthew 17:11, to restore all things for His return.

Malachi 4:5-6 says: "Behold, I am going to send you Elijah the prophet before the coming of the great and terrible day of the Lord. And he will restore the hearts of the fathers to their children, and the hearts of children to their fathers, lest I come and smite the land with a curse." Not long ago the Lord gave us a new depth of understanding about the meaning of restoring the hearts of fathers and children. We spent many years concentrating on family relationships, which is still needed everywhere; but now we should also think about our history, and consider these things:

Jewish people are the fathers; Christians are the children.

Catholics are the fathers; Protestants are the children.

Indigenous people in any lands are the fathers; colonists are the children.

God's call upon us is to bring reconciliation between Jews and Christians, Catholics and Protestants (indeed, all branches of His Body with every other branch), and natives the world over with colonists and Christians.

*What must we do before true reconciliation can happen and Jesus' prayer be answered?* Can we discard our old wineskins, trusting the Lord whenever we start to feel challenged and stretched by others in their cultural ways, and by what they believe? Will we be flexible and renewed enough within ourselves to participate in the revival that is coming to all men, of every race, culture, and creed? Doesn't that requisite magnanimity of heart, flexibility, and willingness to change actually depend upon how much our character has been transformed into His likeness? Thus the pre-requisite need for inner healing if reconciliation is to be fully accomplished.

Though our Lord uses every event in life and all our church participation to transform our natures, it is through inner healing, one for another, that the depth and range of transformation of character actually transpires. We cannot effect reconciliation if what we are and do continues to tear apart the fabric of unity.

## JESUS IS COMING FOR ONE BRIDE, NOT A HAREM!

His Bride must become a resting place for her Husband. "Surely I will not enter my house, nor lie on my bed; I will not give sleep to my eyes, or slumber to my eyelids; until I find a place for the Lord, a dwelling place for the mighty one of Jacob" (Ps. 132:3-5). Our Lord is looking for a people in whom He can relax and rest, who will not err and disgrace His name if He lets down His watchfulness over them for a moment. How can we be that restful place for Him if we are not dead to self and raised anew in Him? Inner transformation is crucial!

Our Lord's Bride must be one whom He can trust. *"The heart of her husband trusts in her, and he will have no lack of gain. She does him good and not evil all the days of her life"* (Prov. 31:11-12).

The Lord's Bride is being cleansed and prepared now. In these days the Body of Christ, wherever people will receive, is experiencing renewal and transformation. Renewal of the faithful has to come before revival of the many. God is preparing us for revival, equipping individuals and groups for what lies ahead. Churches and para-church organizations have been experiencing house cleaning and heart cleansing. Inner healing is thus one of the Holy Spirit's primary tools in His task of preparing the Lord's Bride for His return.

We pray that more and more people, especially born-anew Christians, may catch the vision and see that until hearts are cleansed and transformed, no other work will endure. Only so can the Lord's Bride be made ready, beautified and adorned for His return. Many are seeing the light and beginning to work for the cleansing and maturation of the Body of Christ. Malachi 4:5-6 *promised* that Elijah *will* turn the hearts of fathers and children to each other before the great and terrible day of the Lord arrives. The Holy Spirit is doing a quick work. We look forward with anticipation.

Maranatha! Even so, come, Lord!

CHAPTER TWELVE

# BIRTHING ELIJAH HOUSE

(PAULA)

I n July 1961 we moved from Streator, Illinois, to accept a call to pastor in Council Grove, Kansas. John had received a dream of what to expect there, and before we moved, and after, each part of the dream was confirmed. (Details of this story are described in *The Elijah Task*.)

The call was to the First Congregational Church of the United Church of Christ, having within it a mixture of liberal parishioners and the devoutly biblical. Very soon a prayer group of seasoned Christians developed, as well as a youth group with a passion for Jesus. They were excited that the Lord was answering their prayers, and they worked hard with John to clear land and gather rocks for the building of a church camp on land surrounded on three sides by water from the newly formed Council Grove Reservoir. Some parents complained that we were influencing their teenagers to be religious fanatics, but some years later a parent who had complained let us know that her son was working full time with a national Christian organization. She joyfully said to John, "And it's all your fault!" She was grateful for the training her son had received that equipped him for ministry.

Forty years ago, while we were in Kansas, John and I were invited several times to the university at Lawrence, Kansas, to teach a group of Christian students led by an engineering professor, Dr. Nick Willems. The young men's group was called "The Mustard Seed," and the young women were "The Rib."

Among other biblical truths, we shared what we had learned about inner healing. The professor later combined the two groups as a church and became their pastor. Just recently, he and his wife spent a pleasant week with us in our home in northern Idaho, and visited the healing rooms in Spokane, Washington. Shortly afterward he reported that he was no longer afflicted with asthma. They informed us that the prayer group in Council Grove is still alive and carrying on in the prayer ministry we started so many years ago. What a joy to hear such a report!

We left Council Grove after four and a half years and the birth of our son Timothy. This move was in response to a call to pastor a church in Wallace, Idaho. This time the Holy Spirit gave both John and me clear visions of what to expect there, and all of those visions came to pass. We were warned that we were being sent to "Egypt"; and during our nine years of service in Wallace, we came to understand what that meant! Knowing that we were where the Lord had planted us made it much easier from the beginning to face the difficulties that lay ahead.

There were many experiences to celebrate: good friends, the birth of our daughter Andrea, beautiful scenic mountains and streams, camping, our prayer group, church choirs, Bible studies, children's activities, participation in citywide revival services, and fun as a part of community musical drama productions.

I was recruited by the Superintendent of Schools at Mullan, Idaho, to teach Spanish, English, and Idaho History at the High School. Superintendent John Loveless, who attended the adult Sunday school class I was teaching, discovered I had the required credits in those subjects and experienced firsthand my teaching ability. I enjoyed my teaching position for several years. Then on an early winter day in 1970, as I was driving home down the mountainside, I hit black ice on a curve and flew headfirst through the windshield of my van as it hit the guardrail and rolled. I landed flat on my back on the pavement. However, the Lord did a miraculous job of healing, and I was back at school in a couple of weeks, happy not only to be alive, but grateful for all the help our parishioners had given me. My students also were very considerate and helpful. Later I did a great deal of substitute teaching in the Wallace Junior and Senior High Schools as well.

John and I were often chaperones at weekend school dances where our oldest son Loren's band was playing. The critics in the church who condemned rock and roll and anyone who played it gave Loren and us a bad time, not recognizing that pot and alcohol were banned from the dance halls and that the dances kept the youth off the streets and out of trouble each weekend. Little did they know that God was using Loren's band leadership to train him as a team leader for Christ. Loren went on to major in music and became the composer of many beautiful Christian worship songs—and the worship leader for the first gathering of the Promise Keepers.

Loren is now the pastor of a thriving church in Thornton, Colorado, but when he first came to us wanting to become a rock and roll band leader, we were the pastors of the largest church in the valley— in the day when rock and roll was thought to be of the devil! That put us on the spot. Strangely the Lord said, "You are not only to let him do it, but you are also to back him financially and every other way."

We backed him at the bank with our heart in our throats, but he never missed a payment. God's wisdom was proven; because Loren had to practice hour after hour and was on stage performing each weekend, he never had time to get into the troubles many of his friends fell into! Some may think us foolish, or unchristian, to allow him to do such a thing, but Loren says, "I can now be trusted and belong to God because my parents trusted me when I couldn't be trusted."

Enduring the persecution and standing by Loren taught us much, and became deep lessons that we have in turn taught to many parents about how to raise teenagers—for which many have thanked us over the years. Above all, teenagers need the trust and support of their parents.

Opportunities to minister often come in surprise packages. One of my students had been seriously injured when a deer suddenly jumped out of the woods, landed on him, and knocked him off his motorcycle. The school called me to say that his parents were requesting that I visit him in the hospital because he was refusing to follow the doctor's instructions to remain quiet. They thought he might listen to me. I talked to this boy about the injuries I had suffered in my accident, and the recovery I had experienced because I honored the doctor's instructions and received prayer from people who cared. He heard, allowed me to pray for him, settled down, and soon all was well.

The reference the Lord had made about sending us to Egypt referred to strongholds over the minds of the people in the area. There were five open houses of prostitution with neon lights in this mining town, and bars everywhere. The prevailing attitude of people was that the brothels had always been there and always would be, and that they were needed for the protection of our women and the sake of the area's economy. "Our women would be raped if those houses weren't there"—this despite the fact that year after year social studies students from the University of Idaho conducted scholastic door-to-door surveys of the Wallace population, and found that there was just as much or more rape in our county as anywhere else. The people had developed a "sweep it under the rug" mentality.

We and many others prayed, and finally the government closed the houses. The national TV media made the rounds of the town, asking people what they thought of this action. When the media interviewed John and asked what he thought, he said, "Hallelujah! It's an answer to prayer!" We were then hard hit with persecution, even from some within the church. "You have given our town a bad name!" Our children were ridiculed at school and greatly disillusioned by many of the church members.

We served there nine years until the Lord gave us orders to leave. Recently there has been considerable repentance in the valley among the churches, especially as led by one devout pastor and his church. One of our Elijah House prayer counselors has been loaned to that area to minister as the people are realizing their needs for help.

In addition to pastoring, John was traveling outside of our church to teach four to six times a year. He was also counseling many needy people inside and outside of our church. When our son

Loren was studying at Fuller Seminary, he was given an assignment to write a description of the home he grew up in. One outstanding comment he made was, "I would often come home to find our living room full of living human wreckage—but soon I would see them transformed and made new."

John was always bringing someone home who needed help, and our children followed that example. When John and I returned from a meeting late one evening, we found that our children had welcomed a large van load of college students on their way to Minnesota, had fed them, and bedded them down. The next morning we did some ministry with those young people and privately spoke a word of caution to our own.

We regularly attended a large charismatic prayer meeting at Gonzaga University in Spokane, Washington, where John was an advisor to the leadership. As John related earlier, Bishop Topel of the Catholic Church even gave John his permission and blessing to act as a spiritual director for charismatic nuns in his parish! Occasionally a Spokane psychiatrist would call on him to pray deliverance prayers for those he discerned had need for that kind of prayer but felt he couldn't do in his office. Several in our prayer group were helping, but John was still overloaded. And so he asked the Lord to lessen his load. The Lord was clear when He finally said to John that we were to resign and move 45 miles away to Coeur D'Alene, Idaho, to write, teach, and counsel, in that order. Some people thought we were crazy to make such a move with six children (two of whom were in college, and one in seminary) when we had no money, and no guaranteed income.

Our first book, *The Elijah Task*, tells the complete story of how God acted to enable us, with no money and no job, to purchase a brand new house and move into it within a 24-hour period! This was November of 1973. The real estate agent said he had never seen such a thing happen before, and probably never would again. God was faithful. He brought people for us to counsel, forbade us to charge a set fee, but moved on the hearts of people to give us enough to keep our bills paid and our credit rating healthy.

We continued to pray blessing for those who attacked, and have persevered in pioneering inner healing and the prophetic ministry. In a sense, we give thanks for all the persecution because it did wondrous things for us: It drove us to our knees in constant prayer. It forced us to examine ourselves and to reground everything as carefully as possible in the Bible and sound doctrine. It caused us to love Jesus more fervently as persecution made us so much more keenly aware of what He endured for our sakes. It made us more corporate as we learned to rely on others for correction and reproof lest our attackers' words become true. It increased gratitude in us for courageous people who stand no matter what others think and who put God and His Kingdom first. It taught us to love the unlovable. And it made the pages of the Bible come alive, as we lived in some meager ways what the fathers of the faith suffered at the hands of rebellious and contentious people.

In all this, we tried to protect time that belonged to our children and to keep a healthy balance of activities. We played cards, took camping trips, went huckleberry picking, had picnics, and went bicycling, swimming in the lake, and occasionally roller skating. I learned to be straightforward with people who were demanding of time we had promised to our children.

A woman called one evening to describe her problem and insisted on a next-day appointment. I asked her how long she had had her problem, and she said it had been going on forever. I suggested then that with God's help she could bear it one more day because we had promised to spend the next day with our children—and if we were to break promises to them, someone might have to counsel them someday. She quit her whining, I prayed a short prayer for her, and she settled for an appointment several days later.

When our children were older, we traveled as much as we could to teach wherever we were invited, trying our best for the sake of our children not to be gone too long or too frequently. Bless their hearts—they were very forgiving—but they were not at all happy with the meals served by the woman we arranged to stay with them. They were so good about it that we only found that out years later.

Often when they were younger we were invited to teach at family camps in the summer, and they traveled with us across much of the United States and parts of Canada.

In the following years the number of counselees increased even more. Though John did most of the counseling, sometimes each of us was seeing eight to ten people a day! I remember receiving a request from a very well-known medical doctor who practiced in Spokane. He wanted a counseling appointment but we didn't have an opening for the next three weeks. A few days later his receptionist arrived at our home in the middle of the day to deliver a message, "If we should ever have an *urgent* need for an appendectomy, he certainly would not make us wait for three weeks!" We understood the urgency and made room for him in the late evening. We are happy to say that he was ripe for healing and experienced a wonderful transformation that was evident and very much appreciated in his work relationships and at home. He even became a speaker for the Full Gospel Businessmen's Association.

Before long we added several other counselors to minister in our home in addition to ourselves. We also had a staff person working in the basement packaging and mailing books and cassette tapes, and processing handwritten, mimeographed copies of a periodic newsletter. Some of our neighbors began to complain about the increased traffic on our street and the lack of parking space.

We were no longer able to enjoy any privacy in our home, and our children were beginning to be only patiently and politely enduring. Each evening as we sat down to dinner we could count on the phone's ringing before our derrieres hit our chairs. One afternoon our son Tim's girlfriend Victoria (now for many years his wife) knew none of us was available to answer the phone, so she did it for us.

"Is Mrs. Sandford there?"

"No, I'm sorry she isn't."

"Well, where is she?"

"I think she's at the grocery store."

"What? Do you mean to tell me Mrs. Sandford actually shops for groceries!?"

"Of course she does. If she didn't, her family would starve."

Just as Victoria said that, she looked down—and discovered she was standing smack dab in the middle of the kitty litter box. We've been chuckling over that ever since. We pray that people will always know us as ordinary people with an extraordinary God.

Many of those who came seeking prayer ministry were very helpful. When we were harvesting food from our garden, they would volunteer to snap beans, shell peas, and even go home with red hands from peeling beets. One day a group presented me with a huge pressure canner. Another day several arrived with canning jars when those were scarce. Almost everyone prayed blessing on our garden—and the garden went crazy. We were the only ones we ever heard of to have nine pickings of peas from one planting! A man from Illinois bought us a trampoline as a thank you to our children for allowing us to come to teach in his church. Now our grandchildren and great-grandchildren enjoy his gift as well.

Then came the time when a builder, who attended the church our son Loren pastored, contacted us, telling us he knew we needed more space. Due to recession in the area he had been unable to sell a house he had just completed in Hayden Lake, and he couldn't afford to carry it any longer, paying interest at the bank. He said he wanted to move to Alaska where he could find work and a better market and so he would sell the house to us at what it had cost him to build. It took an amazingly short time to arrange that, and just in time for Thanksgiving we gratefully moved into the house where we still live today.

Our longtime friends, Ken and Donna Campbell, who had been hard hit by the recession in the Silver Valley when the mines and smelter closed, consented to move into the house we had just vacated—Ken to handle Elijah House business, and Donna to schedule appointments and serve as receptionist and housekeeper.

After a few years Ken, who had been very successful in real estate previous to the recession, found an ideal piece of property in nearby Post Falls. John had told Ken in 1984 that he should be on the lookout for property suitable for a growing ministry such as ours.

Ken says that many times driving by, seeing this place from the highway, he had thought it would be ideal; but at that time Elijah House was not in a position to purchase because the owner, who was a farmer wanting to retire, was asking $300,000. Ken thought that if only the property would be split up, we might be able to do something.

Two or three years later at Cornerstone Church (where our son Loren was pastor), Ken was talking to a couple who were working in real estate, telling them what we would like. They told him that the Richards' property in Post Falls was up for sale again. Between 1984 and 1987 the property had sold twice, but each time the deal had fallen through.

In 1988 Ken entered into an agreement with the Richards, and for only $1000 down got an option to buy. That option allowed us over a period of years to purchase the property parcel by parcel.

The house on that property had been built as a spacious home for a family with seven children—seven bedrooms, four bathrooms, large living room, dining room, and kitchen, two stone fireplaces, full basement, and garage. A barn stands down the lane. The Spokane River runs by our 70+ acres, with about 850 feet of river front (fulfillment of a prophecy from Dick Mills many years before, that we would have property by water). At present the property with its improvements is worth well over a million dollars and we only owe approximately two hundred thousand dollars! To us this is one of God's precious miracles. Ken and Donna lived there and continued to serve, he as our CEO and caretaker and she as our telephone person who scheduled appointments and answered mail, until their retirement. Jeff Guyett then became our CEO, and our office staff grew and eventually departmentalized.

The new Elijah House property at first housed our office staff and work rooms on the basement level and our receptionist and prayer ministers on the ground level. Very soon, though, we were in need of much more room for prayer counselors and office staff. We looked into the cost of building and found that we could not get fire insurance for the size of building we needed unless we would first create a 500,000 gallon reservoir tank or lake, at enormous cost to us. Then one day, Catholic friends, Bob and Rosemarie Helling from California, approached John at a seminar, saying that they had a large gift they would like to give us.

Having had many such offers before that had fizzled as nothing but, good intentions, John simply said, "Well, thanks," and walked away. Then he nearly fainted when Bob persisted and said they wanted to donate $50,000 to erect six small cottages, five for counseling offices and one for a rest room. He and his sons who were a construction team, would come to Idaho and build them for us! The insurance company informed us that small cottages like that could be insured. We were amazed, delighted, and very grateful for the beauty of the little cottages. Since then, as the need has grown, we have constructed two more cottages with the wonderful help of The Mappers (a group of retired people who come with their RVs, live on the property, and build for Christian organizations).

Total Numbers of People (and Their Home Countries) Receiving Individual Intensive Week-long Prayer Ministry at Elijah House in Post Falls, Idaho in **2001 ALONE**: Australia – 2, Austria – 1, Bermuda – 2, Canada – 19, England – 3, Germany – 3, Hong Kong – 2, Ireland – 1, Italy – 1, Japan – 2, Mexico – 13, Russia – 1, Singapore – 4, Taiwan – 2, USA – 588.

A breakdown of people receiving ministry by home state or province that year is: Alaska – 8, Arizona – 5, California – 88, Colorado – 9, Washington D.C. - 2, Florida – 34, Georgia – 3, Hawaii -3, Idaho -66, Illinois – 9, Indiana – 3, Iowa -3, Kansas – 2, Kentucky – 2, Maine – 1, Maryland – 2, Massachusetts – 8, Michigan – 24, Minnesota – 5, Montana -22, Nebraska – 3, Nevada – 16, New Jersey – 4, New Mexico – 6, New York – 3, North Carolina – 10, Ohio – 4, Oklahoma – 16, Oregon – 21, Pennsylvania – 10, South Dakota – 3, North Dakota – 2, Tennessee – 12, Texas – 18, Utah – 10, Vermont – 1, Virginia – 9, Washington – 134, Wisconsin – 3, Wyoming – 4, Alberta – 4, British Columbia – 4, Manitoba – 2, Nova Scotia – 2, Ontario – 3, Saskatchewan – 4.

Many hundreds more have received individual ministry from Elijah House people who traveled around the world to teach that year, and from those who have shared what they have received with those at home. The total number of people ministered to in over 28 years of Elijah House's existence numbers in the hundreds of thousands. We've lost count.

Over the years, we have redesigned and enlarged the entryway to the main building, turned the garage into a meeting room and the former breezeway into two offices. A lovely guest house has been built on the hill south of the main house, and a sixplex is in process of construction. Both overlook a small lake that we've rejuvenated. It is filled by water pumped from the river, and is refreshed by a little waterfall. (A neighborhood moose was the first to dip his feet into it.) Deer and elk are often seen there and an eagle occasionally flies by. The lake also fulfilled requirements for fire protection in case we receive enough funds to build a larger building.

A part of the initial vision for Elijah House included a place where people, especially pastors and leaders, could come to be rejuvenated physically as well as emotionally and spiritually, and guests have told us that the beauty of the property, with its trees and mountains all around, is therapeutic in itself. When we have the funds and the sixplex is completed, we will have much more ability to provide rest for the weary and disheartened. Many pastors have experienced burnout and quit. When pastors abandon a God-given calling, nothing goes right for them after that because they wander down a desert track while the river of the Lord's blessing for them flows elsewhere. That doesn't have to happen, and the situation is redeemable. We look for the day when we can offer free lodging for the Lord's wounded warriors.

Through the donations of many Elijah House supporters, we have been able to pave 1,300 feet of our driveway, enough for us to reach the county road, a great help especially in winter.

Elijah House land had been originally owned by the Coeur D'Alene Indians, and one day we were wonderfully blessed when a family from the tribe came to pray blessing for us and the land. They joined in our Thursday morning prayer time and then we went out-side. They welcomed us to the land, and spoke with authority to any powers of darkness that might be opposing us, directing them to leave in the name of Jesus, now that Elijah House had been granted full authority over our land.

And then that lovely Indian lady, Wilma Bobb, prayed blessing for us and the land as we shared Holy Communion together and she poured what was left of the grape juice into the ground. We em-braced one another, shared a few gifts, and went out to lunch to-gether. Since that day, there has been a remarkable difference in the atmosphere of the property, a sense of lightness and joy, comfort and safety.

## Reaching Out

John and I had realized very early that alone we could never reach enough of the population to make a significant difference in the Body of Christ, even though our books have become best-sellers and thousands of videos and cassettes have spread throughout the land. The Lord spoke to us to say that most ministries die along with the founders, but that was not to happen to Elijah House. He gave us Ephesians 4:11 and told us we needed to teach people how to minis-ter to one another and to raise up people, first in administration, and then in prayer ministry and teaching, to replace us and carry on eventually without us.

For a while, we hosted weekend seminars in Spokane where we taught biblical principles of confession, repentance, cleansing the heart, forgiveness, rebirth, sanctification, transformation, renewal of the mind, love, blessing, etc. Teaching those who came how to gath-er together in small groups to become honest with one another, and to pray for one another, yielded tremendously good fruit, and people came from nearby states, Canadian provinces, and even from as far away as Germany to experience and learn. People who were familiar with small group ministry in our son Loren's church in Post Falls served as group leaders.

We began to see more and more that ours is a ministry of *healing hearts and changing lives*, which has become the title of the quarterly magazine we publish. At first most of the people who came for the seminars were lay people. Then more pastors began to come, and then a number of psychologists and psychiatrists. The latter said they knew a lot about diagnosing people's problems and had learned many helpful techniques, but were recognizing that only God can heal. They wanted to know how to pray to reach the deep levels of the heart. Many reported to us later that when they were allowed to pray for their clients, healing happened much faster than before.

At those seminars, we never wrote more information than first names on name tags because we found that many of the professionals were expected to have all the answers, or do all of the work in their group—or they thought they were—which destroyed the effectiveness of the small group. They needed to relate as ordinary persons.

Once, in those early days, when we held a seminar full of pastors and professional counselors, we found that every group was simply fizzling—none were truly sharing themselves. The Lord revealed to us that as adults they had reached a level of feeling competent, able to help others. Therefore they did not want to become childlike again—associated in their minds with weakness, vulnerability, and hurt. They could feel expansive and noble listening compassionately to the hurts of others, but didn't want to talk about the wounds and sins of their own childhood. Consequently, very little was happening in their small groups. We talked about the lack of sharing in the general gathering, prayed about it as the Holy Spirit led, and cast away fear, praying for restoration of trust in wounded hearts. Quite a few began to open their hearts, becoming real and vulnerable with each other, and healing ministry resulted.

As time went on we realized that we needed more than a weekend to enable people to learn new ways of thinking, ministering, and praying. We found that most were coming to receive ministry rather than to learn how to help others, and even those who wanted to learn to minister had deeply ingrained ways of going about it. They would hear a lesson, and then instead of practicing the new way of ministering we were teaching, they would flip back to their old familiar ways that didn't work.

At that time many people in the Body of Christ were habitually shouting at demons, not realizing that often they were trying to cast out what were really character and personality complexes and traits. Or they were saying things like, "Come on now, you don't want to feel that way." Or, "Cheer up, it isn't that bad." Or, "You think you had it bad, let me tell you what happened to me." We decided we would have to change the three-day program into a three-week school. We saw we needed time to overcome and break down the old failing methods they came with, and build in the new. And it worked!

The first school was held at Cornerstone Church in Post Falls, and people came from far distances. One of those was Dr. Rolph Senst who is now head of Ignis Psychiatric Clinic in Altensteig, Germany. He became our translator for many of the early seminars we conducted in Germany. Another was Myra Wilkinson, who went home to found Elijah House Australia.

At the next school, in New Windsor, Maryland, Carol Arnott came and then went home to train 50 people who became the team that prayed for people when renewal broke out in Toronto Airport Church on January 20, 1994. Most of the people who have attended our schools have turned out to be fertile seeds for ministry growth, and many have taken what they learned to their churches and encouraged others to come to receive Elijah House training.

At our schools we include worship, teaching, small group ministry, and a number of demonstrations of the way we counsel. For these we need volunteers. At a school we held in Fresno, California, a tall, quiet, dignified gentleman with only his first name printed on his name tag offered himself for the demonstration. He didn't appear to have any deep complicated problems, but was relaxed, open, honest, and humble in the way he answered our questions. He received inner healing prayer very well with a grateful heart, a good example for the rest of the students. We liked what we felt in his spirit. After the session John and I asked him what he did for a living when he wasn't attending a school. He said he was a pastor. We asked, "Where?" He responded, "Hollywood Presbyterian." This was Lloyd Ogilvie, who later became chaplain of the US Senate!

Presently we offer what we call "live schools" and "video schools." A few years ago Melody Green (widow of Keith Green and cofounder of Last Days Ministries) called us to say that if we would hold a live school for the people at Last Days Ministries at no cost to them, they would employ three professional cameramen and videotape everything for us for only the cost of the tapes! We enjoyed the venture. Since that time, video schools have been held in many churches across the country and around the world with certified graduates from our live schools acting as facilitators.

ATTENDANCE NUMBERS FOR OUR SCHOOLS FROM 1988-2001:

—Students attending basic live schools in the U.S.A. — 1,671

—Students attending advanced schools in the U.S.A — 680

—Students attending video schools in the U.S.A. — 5,841

—Correspondent students — 536

—Total U.S. school students — 8,728

—Total U.S. school graduates — 6,344

—International basic live school students — 1,030

—Total international school graduates — 725


Grand Total Elijah House School Students — 9,758

Elijah House School Graduates — 7,069


Another opportunity to learn is through seminars we call "KEYS." These are offered periodically and focus on healing in small groups.

## ELIJAH HOUSE'S INTERNSHIP PROGRAM

When we refer to "Elijah House counselors," we are not referring to secular counseling, though some of our staff have received that sort of training also. We are referring to those who do pastoral counseling based on biblical principles, common sense, and Holy Spirit-led prayer. What we do should properly be called "prayer counseling."

When students have graduated from the basic and advanced Elijah House Schools, they may apply for an internship.

**Internship Overview:** Elijah House internship is patterned after Jesus' example of discipleship—watch another do it; do it together; do it yourself; then go and train others to do it.

**Internship I** (Duration: 13 weeks)
—One week of receiving intensive counseling (15 hours)
—Four weeks of observing
—Eight weeks of co-counseling
—Counseling-related projects assigned as needed

**Internship II** (Duration: 12 weeks)
—Nine weeks of co-counseling
—Three weeks of supervised independent counseling (which is a ratio of one supervised independent week for every three of co-counseling)
—Counseling-related projects assigned as needed

**Internship III** (Duration: 24 weeks)
—Eighteen weeks of supervised independent counseling
—Six weeks of co-counseling (again a ratio of three to one)
—Counseling-related projects required
—Opportunity to supervise other interns and possibly to teach training materials.

Interns observe and co-counsel with each one of the staff counselors, learning how each ministers according to the same biblical principles, flavored and enhanced by their own different personalities and gifting. Interns will be declared ready to advance as they receive approval from department head Rob Morrisett, and those who are already on staff. Some may complete a time of residency to become a part of our staff.

We have established Elijah Houses in other parts of the world as well—Canada, Australia, Austria, Finland, and New Zealand. We also expect to add Elijah Houses in South Africa and Japan as well.

**Elijah House Task Force Regional Contacts in the United States are:**

**Pacific Northwest:** AK, WA ,OR, ID, MT, WY—Jeff and Cheri Hansen

**Northwest Central:** ND, SD, NE, MN, IA, WI—Gary and Ethel Horton

**Northeast Central:** IL, IN, OH, MI—Joan Feikema/Pete Chandler, The Healing Tree

**Central Atlantic:** MD, DE, NC, KY, VA, WV—Lawana G. Atkins, Greensprings Chapel

**New England:** NY, CT, RI, MA, VT, NH, ME, PA, NJ—H. Robert Stoppard, Breath of Life Ministries

**Pacific Southwest:** CA, NV, AZ, UT, HI—Bridget E. Shank Desert Gardens

**Central Mountain:** CO, NM, KS, OK—Glee Myrant, The Vineyard on Smoky Hill Road

**Southeast:** MS, AL, GA, FL, TN, SC—Richard and Virginia Robinson, Oaks of Righteousness, Inc.

**For General ETF Information:** Bonnie Hartley, ETF Communications Coordinator, 206-246-0587, FAX 206-246-9004, or email: ETF@macconnect.com

## A WORD OF ENCOURAGEMENT FROM MARK RUNNELS

**(Part of the Bloomington, Minnesota, Assembly of God Church as a Counselor/Teacher)**

"It was wonderful to have John and Paula here with us at Bloomington Assembly of God last month. On Friday afternoon they met with the Elijah Task Force for an informal time of fellowship and prayer. John mentioned that they are at an age when they thought they would retire, but that God had told them otherwise. They said that God told them that much more would be accomplished in and through their lives. Seeing and hearing them speak Friday night and all day Saturday left no doubt in my mind. The same energy, the same anointing is still there that I have seen in them the last eleven years that I have been exposed to them and their materials. In fact, there seemed to be a greater joy in their lives than I have ever seen before. It was fun to have them here. I want to share something that I think God showed to me while they were here. Please pass it along to them if you find any merit in it at all.

"About thirty minutes after they walked into the prayer room at Bloomington Assembly to meet with the Elijah Task Force, I began seeing a storm. The storm was above them but they were unaffected by it. I saw black, rolling storm clouds that were moving swiftly as if blown by strong winds. I kept seeing this scene over and over while we were meeting with them that afternoon. [John and I, Paula, had received a word from the Lord years before—that we would someday be rocks in a sea of chaos.]

"I had a repeat of this picture that evening and throughout the next day while they were teaching. But a new picture was added to what I had seen the day before. In the new picture I could see a very high rock formation to my left. Looking up at the sky above, I could see a powerful wind that was blowing from left to right. The rock was blocking the wind from affecting me. The wind was so strong that I could actually see it. Perhaps it was sand or some type of debris I was seeing in the wind. It sort of reminded me of the sandstorms you could see in the old cowboy movies. It was blowing at an incredible speed but was not affecting anyone on the ground—just like John and Paula were unaffected by the black storm clouds above their heads. I kept seeing these two pictures throughout the day; first I would see one and then I would see the other.

"Three days later I read Isaiah 32 as my daily devotion. Verse two really caught my attention. 'Each man will be like a shelter from the wind and a refuge from the storm, like streams of water in the desert, and the shadow of a great rock in a thirsty land.' I don't know how to interpret all of this. Isaiah 32 certainly describes what John and Paula's ministry has been to so very many people. Within the context of Isaiah 32, this verse also describes perhaps the most important impact Elijah House has had on the body of Christ—raising 'each man' to minister to the body of Christ.

"Verse one says, 'See, a king will reign in righteousness and rulers will rule with justice.' Of course Christ is the King spoken of in this verse. The rulers of righteousness would include those of you at Elijah House who are equipping the saints for body ministry. And 'each man' speaks of people like me and others who minister to one another.

"Nothing in this seems to me like fresh revelation to John, Paula, and the rest of you at Elijah House. Perhaps you see something in this that I don't. But I hope it is, at the very least, another confirmation that what you are doing is in the center of God's will for your lives and for the body of Christ."

## A WORD FROM THE AUTHORS

Our former pastor, Bruce Miles, used to tell us frequently that what validated our ministry more than anything else to him, was the character and maturity of our six children, the kind of people they are, and the gifting the Lord has given each one of them (all six being devout Holy Spirit-filled Christians).

A prophetic word spoken over us recently by a gifted prophet was, "And there shall be many more sons and many more daughters which shall come forth from out of your loins, for now I give you this multiplication anointing because through your sons and your daughters they shall now reproduce...." God is so good! We already see this happening in our many children and grandchildren. And we are blessed to be thought of as "Mom and Dad" by an increasing number of spiritual children as well. This ministry will not die with its founders.

# PUBLICATIONS BY MEMBERS OF THE SANDFORD FAMILY

## BOOKS

**by John:**
> *Healing the Nations*
> *Elijah Among Us*
> *Why Some Christians Commit Adultery*

**by John and Paula:**
> *The Elijah Task*
> *Restoring the Christian Family*
> *Transformation of the Inner Man*
> *Healing the Wounded Spirit*

**by Paula:**
> *Healing Victims of Sexual Abuse*
> *Healing Women's Emotions*

**by John and Paula and Lee Bowman (Paula's brohter):**
> *Waking the Slumbering Spirit*
> *Choosing Forgiveness*

**by John and son Loren:**
> *Renewal of the Mind*

**by John and son Mark:**
> *A Comprehensive Guide to Deliverance and Inner Healing*

**by Loren:**
> *A Season of Tens* (The Movement of God in the Millenium)
> *Prophetic Worship*
> *Burnout* (Renewal in the Wilderness)

## BOOKLETS

**by Paula:**
> *New Life for Your Adopted Child*
> *Introduction to Inner Healing*
> *What About Divorce?*
> *Into and Out of the Fog* (Healing for Dyslexia)

**by Beth (Loren's wife):**
> *Meet My Dad*